GAO

Report to the Chairman, Committee on Homeland Security and Governmental Affairs, U.S. Senate

February 2013

IRAN

I0448383

U.S. and International Sanctions Have Adversely Affected the Iranian Economy

GAO
Accountability * Integrity * Reliability

Highlights of GAO-13-326, a report to the Chairman, Committee on Homeland Security and Governmental Affairs, U.S. Senate

February 2013

IRAN

U.S. and International Sanctions Have Adversely Affected the Iranian Economy

Why GAO Did This Study

Since 1987, the United States has implemented a broad range of sanctions targeting Iran to deter it from developing its nuclear program, supporting terrorism, and continuing its human rights abuses. Beginning in 2010, Congress has enacted additional financial sanctions which generally restrict Iranian access to the U.S. financial system. In addition, the United Nations and the European Union have adopted several sanctions to compel Iran to suspend its nuclear program. However, concerns have been raised in Congress and by the United Nations about the impact of these sanctions, including the effect of recent financial sanctions on exports of humanitarian goods to Iran. The export of certain humanitarian goods to Iran is allowed by U.S. law, under certain conditions.

In this report, GAO (1) describes recent laws and executive orders that have added to Treasury's authority to implement financial sanctions targeting Iran, (2) describes U.S. efforts to administer and enforce the financial sanctions, and (3) analyzes evidence of the effect that recent U.S. and international sanctions have had on the Iranian economy. GAO reviewed U.S. public laws, executive orders, and agency guidance; met with U.S. agency officials; and analyzed trade and economic data from the International Monetary Fund, European Union, and others, as well as forecasts of Iran's future economic performance.

View GAO-13-326. For more information, contact Thomas Melito at (202) 512-9601 or melitot@gao.gov.

What GAO Found

Since 2010, congressional legislation, such as the Comprehensive Iran Accountability, Sanctions, and Divestment Act of 2010 (CISADA), as well as a number of executive orders, have established additional U.S. financial sanctions targeting Iran. For example, CISADA authorized the imposition of sanctions on foreign financial institutions that facilitated certain activities or financial transactions by entities including Iran's Islamic Revolutionary Guard Corps. According to an Under Secretary of the Treasury, CISADA "set a new precedent," because "[i]t gave the Secretary of the Treasury the authority for the first time to require U.S. banks to terminate correspondent banking relationships with foreign banks that knowingly engaged in significant transactions with designated Iranian banks."

The Department of the Treasury (Treasury)—along with other U.S government agencies—administers and enforces U.S. financial sanctions targeting Iran. Treasury administers the sanctions by developing regulations, conducting outreach to domestic financial regulators and foreign banks, identifying apparent sanctions violations, and assessing the effects of the sanctions. State administers some investment and trade sanctions, principally energy sanctions, targeting Iran. U.S agencies and federal and state banking regulators have taken a range of actions to ensure compliance with financial sanctions. Specifically, in recent years, Treasury and the Department of Justice (Justice) have taken actions against banks for systematic and willful violations of sanctions laws, including violations of U.S. financial sanctions regulations targeting Iran. For example, in 2012, Justice announced that both HSBC Holdings, PLC and HSBC Bank USA NA had agreed to forfeit $1.256 billion to the United States in connection with violations of sanctions targeting Iran, among other countries.

The combination of U.S. and international sanctions has adversely affected the Iranian economy and its future outlook. According to GAO's analysis, the Iranian economy has consistently underperformed the economies of comparable peer countries across a number of key economic indicators since 2010, when recent sanctions were enacted. In contrast to its peers, Iran's oil production, oil export revenues, and economic growth estimates have fallen, and its inflation has increased. For example, Iran's oil export revenues fell by 18 percent from 2010 to 2012, while its peers' oil export revenues increased by 50 percent. In addition, professional and International Monetary Fund forecasts of the Iranian economy were downgraded to reflect deterioration in Iran's expected economic performance after the implementation of recent sanctions. Some experts have stated that Iran's recent economic deterioration has resulted from a combination of sanctions and Iranian economic mismanagement. GAO's analysis of European Union and U.S. exports to Iran of humanitarian goods indicates that exports of these goods, such as agricultural goods and medicines, increased in the first 10 months of 2012 compared with 2011. UN reports have raised concerns about the availability of such goods in Iran. According to open sources, the government of Iran has tried to adapt to the sanctions through various means, including using alternative payment mechanisms such as barter agreements and changing its trading partners. However, these recent agreements have thus far not fully offset the reduced exports of oil to the European Union and others.

_____ **United States Government Accountability Office**

Contents

Figures

United States Government Accountability Office
Washington, DC 20548

February 25, 2013

The Honorable Thomas R. Carper
Chairman
Committee on Homeland Security
    and Governmental Affairs
United States Senate

Dear Mr. Chairman:

Since 1987, the United States has imposed a broad range of sanctions targeting Iran, such as financial, trade, and investment sanctions, that are intended to deter it from expanding its nuclear program, supporting terrorism, and continuing its human rights abuses. From July 2010 to December 2012, Congress passed legislation that imposed additional financial sanctions that restricted Iran from accessing the U.S. financial system. The Department of the Treasury (Treasury), Department of State (State), and Department of Justice (Justice) administer and enforce these U.S. financial sanctions, and federal and state banking regulators ensure effective compliance with the sanctions programs by the banks that they regulate. The United Nations (UN) and the international community have also been concerned about Iran's nuclear program since the discovery in 2002 that Iran had concealed its nuclear activities for years in breach of its international obligations. Since 2006, the UN has adopted sanctions targeting Iran in an effort to compel it to suspend the development of uranium enrichment and the expansion of its nuclear program. However, concerns have been raised in Congress about the impact of U.S. and international financial sanctions on Iran's economy. In addition, the UN has reported concerns about whether sanctions have limited exports of food and medicine to Iran. U.S. law and regulations allow the export of certain agricultural commodities, food, medicine, and medical devices (which we refer to as "humanitarian goods" in this report) to Iran under certain conditions.[1]

---

[1] 22 U.S.C. § 7201-7211. See also, 31 C.F.R. § 560.530

GAO-13-326 Iran

In response to your request that we examine financial sanctions targeting Iran enacted since 2010, this report (1) describes the recent laws and executive orders that have added to Treasury's authority to implement financial sanctions targeting Iran; (2) describes U.S. efforts to administer and enforce these financial sanctions; and (3) analyzes evidence of the effect that recent U.S. and international sanctions have had on the Iranian economy. (In addition, as agreed with your staff, app. IV provides open-source information on Iran's nuclear program.)

To describe the recent laws and executive orders that have added to Treasury's authority to administer financial sanctions targeting Iran, we reviewed the public laws and executive orders that define these sanctions as well as the regulations developed to implement them. We also reviewed the financial sanctions targeting Iran that the UN, European Union (EU), and other countries have enacted. To review U.S. agencies' efforts to administer and enforce recent U.S. financial sanctions targeting Iran, we reviewed Treasury regulations and guidance establishing the process for administering the sanctions. We interviewed banking regulators and bank representatives to determine the process required for banks to comply with financial sanctions.[2] We also reviewed data on the enforcement of financial sanctions, including enforcement actions and the designation of entities owned or controlled by or acting on behalf of Iran. To analyze evidence of the effect of recent U.S. and international sanctions have had on the Iranian economy, we interviewed U.S. government officials, as well as academic and independent experts, regarding the extent to which sanctions targeting Iran have affected the

---

[2]For the purposes of this report, we use the term "regulators" to refer collectively to the federal regulators of depository institutions, including banks, thrifts, and federally chartered credit unions. The federal banking regulators are the Office of the Comptroller of the Currency, the Board of Governors of the Federal Reserve System, the Federal Deposit Insurance Corporation, and the National Credit Union Administration. The federal banking regulators are responsible for overseeing the various banking entities operating in the United States, including foreign branch offices of U.S. banks. The regulators are also charged with chartering (Office of the Comptroller of the Currency and National Credit Union Administration), insuring (Federal Deposit Insurance Corporation), regulating, and supervising banks. The specific regulatory configuration depends on the type of charter the depository institution chooses. Banks are regulated at the federal level alone if they are chartered by a federal regulator, such as the Office of the Comptroller of the Currency, or by federal and state banking regulators if they are state-chartered institutions. State banking regulators supervise commercial and savings banks with state bank charters, while the Board of Governors of the Federal Reserve System or the Federal Deposit Insurance Corporation, or both, serves as the primary federal regulator for these institutions.

Iranian economy and government and have affected trade with Iran. To assess the performance of the Iranian economy, we analyzed data for several key macroeconomic variables from international trade, energy, and financial data sources, and we compared Iran's performance with that of a select group of peer countries. In addition, we reviewed independent forecasts of the Iranian economy, developed in 2010 and 2012, to identify changes in the predicted future performance of the Iranian economy. In most instances we did not attempt to isolate the impact of U.S. financial sanctions. The contemporaneous implementation of many sanctions, including U.S., UN, and EU financial and non-financial sanctions, would make attributing certain outcomes to any particular sanction very difficult. We met with several business officials in Dubai, United Arab Emirates–a significant exporter of goods to Iran–to discuss the effect that sanctions have had on business with Iran and the resulting impact on Iranian citizens. We also analyzed trade data to assess changes in Iranian trade since 2010 and the effect of sanctions on exports of humanitarian goods to Iran from select countries. Appendix I contains a more detailed description of our scope and methodology. We conducted this performance audit from February 2012 to February 2013 in accordance with generally accepted government auditing standards. Those standards require that we plan and perform the audit to obtain sufficient, appropriate evidence to provide a reasonable basis for our findings and conclusions based on our audit objectives. We believe that the evidence obtained provides a reasonable basis for our findings and conclusions based on our audit objectives.

Background

U.S. Government Sanctions Targeting Iran from 1987 to 2010

The U.S. government has imposed numerous sanctions targeting Iran since 1987, in part to deter Iran from supporting terrorism and developing its nuclear program. U.S. laws and executive orders have established a U.S. trade and investment ban targeting Iran, have been used to impose sanctions against foreign entities that support Iranian terrorist organizations or proliferation activities, and have imposed financial sanctions targeting Iran.[3] According to a Treasury official, the U.S. trade

---

[3]Exec. Order No. 13059, 62 Fed. Reg. 44531 (Aug. 19, 1997); Exec. Order No. 13224, 66 Fed. Reg. 49079 (Sept. 23, 2001); Exec. Order No. 13382, 70 Fed. Reg. 38567 (June 28, 2005); Comprehensive Iran Sanctions, Accountability, and Divestment Act of 2010, Pub. L. No. 111-195, 124 Stat. 1312.

and investment ban was aimed at making it more difficult for Iran to procure U.S. goods, services, and technology, including those that could be used for terrorism or proliferation. In 1987, the United States enacted a ban on imports of Iranian goods and services, and in 1995, executive orders banned specified U.S. exports and investment in Iran.[4] These prohibitions apply to U.S. persons, including U.S. companies and their foreign branches.[5] In 1996, Congress enacted the Iran Sanctions Act of 1996 (ISA), which authorized the imposition of sanctions on foreign firms that make certain investments in Iran's energy sector.[6] In ISA, Congress declared that it is the policy of the United States to deny Iran the ability to support acts of international terrorism and to fund the development and acquisition of weapons of mass destruction and the means to deliver them by limiting the development of Iran's ability to explore for, extract, refine, or transport by pipeline its petroleum resources.[7]

Selected UN and International Sanctions and Actions Targeting Iran from 2002 through 2012

The UN and EU, as well as other countries, have also imposed sanctions to pressure Iran to suspend the development of its nuclear program and end its support for terrorism.[8] In 2002, the International Atomic Energy Agency (IAEA) confirmed allegations that Iran was building facilities that could produce fissile material for the development of a nuclear weapon.[9] After Iran failed to suspend its uranium enrichment program in 2006 pursuant to UN Security Council (UNSC) resolution 1696,[10] the UNSC

---

[4]Exec. Order No. 12163, 52 Fed. Reg. 41940 (Oct. 29, 1987), enacted the ban on imports of Iranian goods and services. In March 1995, the President issued Exec. Order No. 12957, 60 Fed. Reg. 14615 (Mar. 15, 1995) prohibiting U.S. involvement with petroleum development in Iran. Exec. Order No. 12959, 60 Fed. Reg. 24757 (May 6, 1995) banned specified exports and investment.

[5]In August 1997, the President signed Exec. Order No. 13059, 62 Fed. Reg. 44531 (Aug. 19, 1997), which consolidated prior executive orders and prohibits virtually all trade and investment activities with Iran by U.S. persons, wherever located.

[6]The act was previously known as the Iran and Libya Sanctions Act of 1996. Pub. L. No. 104-172, 110 Stat. 1541.

[7]Pub. L. No. 104-172, § 3.

[8]Other countries, such as Australia, Canada, and the United Kingdom, have passed unilateral sanctions targeting Iran.

[9]IAEA is an independent agency affiliated with the UN that was established to control and promote the use of atomic energy.

[10]S.C. Res. 1696, U.N. Doc. S/RES/1696 (2006).

adopted resolutions that imposed several sanctions targeting Iran between 2006 and 2010.[11] Following a UNSC determination that Iran had not suspended the development of its nuclear program, the UNSC adopted additional resolutions that imposed sanctions on Iran, including, among others,

- a proliferation-sensitive nuclear and ballistic missile programs-related embargo;

- a ban on the export or procurement of any arms and related material from Iran and a ban on the supply of seven categories, as specified, of conventional weapons and related material to Iran; and

- a travel ban and an assets freeze on designated persons and entities. The assets freeze also applies to any individuals or entities acting on behalf of, or at the direction of, the designated persons and entities, and to entities owned or controlled by the designated persons or entities.

In addition to the UN, the EU has expressed serious and deepening concerns over the Iranian nuclear program, and has imposed sanctions targeting Iran since 2007. Recent sanctions that the EU enacted in 2012 imposed, among other things, restrictive measures on the energy sector, including a phased embargo of Iranian crude oil imports into the EU and financial sanctions against the Central Bank of Iran.[12] Specifically, recalling the potential connection between Iran's revenues derived from its energy sector and the funding of its proliferation-sensitive nuclear activities as underlined in USCR 1929, the sanctions prohibited the import, purchase, and transport of Iranian crude oil and petroleum products by member states. In addition, the EU has enacted targeted financial measures to freeze the assets of persons and entities associated with Iran's nuclear activities.[13] The Council of the European

---

[11]The UNSC resolutions 1737 (2007), 1747 (2007), 1803 (2008), and 1929 (2010) imposed sanctions against Iran in response to the proliferation risks presented by Iran's nuclear program in light of Iran's continuing failure to meet the requirements of IAEA and to comply with the provisions of earlier Security Council resolutions. S.C. Res. 1737, U.N. Doc. S/RES/1737 (2006); S.C. Res. 1747, U.N. Doc. S/RES/1747 (2007); S.C. Res. 1803, U.N. Doc. S/RES/1803 (2008); and S.C. Res. 1929, U.N. Doc. S/RES/1929 (2010).

[12]Council Decision 2012/35/CFSP, 2012 O.J. (L 19) 22.

[13]*Id.*

Union decided on March 15, 2012, to prohibit the provision of specialized financial messaging services to certain persons and entities that are designated by the UN or EU, or have engaged in, supported, or been associated with Iran's proliferation-sensitive nuclear activities or the development of nuclear weapon delivery systems.[14] In response to the council's decision, on May 17, 2012, the Belgium-based Society for Worldwide Interbank Financial Telecommunication (SWIFT) announced it would end all transactions with Iranian banks that had been designated by the EU.[15] Figure 1 identifies selected U.S. and international actions targeting Iran.

---

[14]Council Decision 2012/152/CFSP, 2012 O.J. (L77) 18.

[15]SWIFT is a member-owned cooperative that provides secure international financial messaging services connecting more than 10,000 banking organizations, securities institutions, and corporate customers in 212 countries. The service enables users to exchange automated, standardized financial information. According to SWIFT, it is incorporated under Belgian law and must comply with EU decisions, as confirmed by the Belgian government.

Figure 1: Selected U.S. and International Sanctions Targeting Iran

Directions:
Click button to view desired date range.   (2013 - 2008)   (2007 - 1984)

Selected U.S. government sanctions	2013 to 2008	Selected international actions
• **Jan:** The National Defense Authorization Act of Fiscal Year (FY) 2013 imposed, among its other provisions, new sanctions on the energy, shipping, and ship-building sectors of Iran as well as financial sanctions targeting Iran.	2013	
• **Feb:** Executive Order (EO) 13599 blocked the property of the government of Iran and Iranian financial institutions. • **Apr:** EO 13606 blocked the property, and suspended entry into the United States, of certain persons with respect to grave human rights abuses via information technology by the governments of Iran and Syria. • **May:** EO 13608 prohibited certain transactions with, and suspended entry into the United States of, foreign sanctions evaders of foreign sanctions with respect to Iran and Syria. • **July:** EO 13622 authorized additional sanctions with respect to Iran, including sanctions on a foreign financial institution that has knowingly conducted any significant transaction for the purchase of petroleum from Iran. • **Aug:** The Iran Threat Reduction and Syria Human Rights Act of 2012 (TRA) was enacted to strengthen Iran sanctions laws for the purpose, among others, of compelling Iran to abandon its pursuit of nuclear weapons and other threatening activities. • **Oct:** EO 13628 authorized the implementation of certain sanctions set forth in the TRA and imposed additional sanctions with respect to Iran, including prohibiting a foreign firm that is owned or controlled by a U.S. person from engaging in certain activities in which the U.S. person is prohibited from engaging.	2012	• **Jan:** The European Union (EU) adopted a council decision establishing an oil embargo on Iran and freezing the assets of the Iranian Islamic Revolutionary Guard Corps. • **Mar:** The EU adopted a council decision prohibiting the provision of specialized financial messaging services to sanctioned Iranian banks. • **June:** The United Nations Security Council (UNSC) resolution 2049 renewed the mandate of the Panel of Experts established by resolution 1929 for 13 months. • **Oct:** The EU adopted a council decision that broadened the restrictive measures against Iran adopted in July 2010.
• **May:** EO 13574 authorized Department of the Treasury (Treasury) to implement certain sanctions as set forth in the Iran Sanctions Act of 1996, as amended. • **Nov:** EO 13590 authorized the imposition of certain sanctions with respect to the provision of goods, services, technology, or support for Iran's energy and petrochemical sectors. • **Dec:** The National Defense Authorization Act for FY 2012, Section 1245, designated Iran's financial sector a primary money-laundering concern and directed the President to block the assets of Iranian financial institutions.	2011	
• **July:** The Comprehensive Iran Sanctions, Accountability, and Divestment Act of 2010 added Iranian sanctions in the areas of refined petroleum sales, serious human rights abuses, and access to the U.S. financial system and revoked general authorization to import certain foodstuffs and carpets from Iran. • **Sept:** EO 13553, among its other actions, blocked the property of certain persons with respect to serious human rights abuses by the government of Iran.	2010	• **June:** UNSC resolution 1929, among its other provisions, required that members prevent the transfer of ballistic missile technology to Iran; froze the funds and assets of the Islamic Revolutionary Guard Corps and the Islamic Republic of Iran Shipping Lines; called on members to prohibit Iranian banks from opening new branches in their territories if they have reasonable grounds to believe that these activities could contribute to Iran's nuclear activities; and requested the creation of a Panel of Experts to assist in implementing measures in resolution 1737. • **July:** The EU, in implementing resolution 1929, adopted a council decision establishing restrictions on the transfer of funds to and from Iran and restrictions on the establishment of branches and subsidiaries of Iranian banks.
	2009	
	2008	• **Mar:** UNSC resolution 1803, among its other provisions, required members to generally prevent certain persons designated as providing support for Iran's proliferation sensitive nuclear activities from entering into, or transiting through, their territories; called upon members to exercise vigilance over the activities of financial institutions in their territories with all banks domiciled in Iran; required members to prevent the supply of certain items related to nuclear programs to Iran; and called upon members to inspect, consistent with law and agreements, certain cargoes to and from Iran. • **Sept:** UNSC resolution 1835 called upon Iran to comply with prior resolutions to suspend all enrichment-related and reprocessing activities fully and without delay.

Source: GAO analysis of U.S. laws and executive orders, as well as UN documents, including UN Security Council resolutions.

 **Print instructions** | • Click button for desired date range. In "Print" dialog box, choose "Current view," then "OK." Repeat for each view.
• A print version of this graphic, showing both date ranges, is available in appendix II.

U.S. Law Allows Exports of Humanitarian Goods to Iran

U.S. law allows the export of certain agricultural goods, medicine, and medical devices to Iran under certain conditions.[16] The Trade Sanctions Reform and Export Enhancement Act of 2000 (TSRA) required the President to terminate any unilateral agricultural or medical sanction.[17] In addition, some of the laws and executive orders authorizing U.S. sanctions targeting Iran include language that allows for certain exceptions to the sanctions, such as for agricultural goods or medicine.[18] For the purposes of this report, we refer to agricultural goods, medicine, and medical devices that are authorized for export to Iran as "humanitarian goods."

Treasury's Office of Foreign Assets Control (OFAC) issues licenses that authorize the export and reexport of humanitarian goods pursuant to TSRA. OFAC indicated that it provides exporters with an efficient and expedited process to export humanitarian goods.

---

[16]Trade Sanctions Reform and Export Enhancement Act of 2000, Pub. L. No. 106-387, Title IX, 114 Stat. 1549, 1549A-67 – 1549A-72 (codified as amended at 22 U.S.C. §§ 7201-7211).

[17]22 U.S.C. § 7202(b). TSRA defined agricultural commodities by referencing the meaning given to that term in section 102 of the Agricultural Trade Act of 1978, and defined medicine and medical devices by adopting the definitions of drug and device set forth in section 201 of the Federal Food, Drug, and Cosmetic Act.

[18]For example, National Defense Authorization Act for Fiscal Year 2012, Pub. L. No. 112-81, § 1245, 125 Stat. 1298, 1647-1650 (2011) and Exec. Order No. 13622, § 1(d), 77 Fed. Reg. 45897 (Aug. 2, 2012).

From 2010 through 2012, the United States Established Additional Financial Sanctions Targeting Iran

Comprehensive Iran Sanctions Accountability and Divestment Act

Recent congressional legislation and a number of executive orders enacted since 2010 have established additional U.S. financial sanctions targeting Iran.[19] According to Treasury, recent U.S. financial sanctions targeting Iran are authorized by, and outlined in, four laws and a number of executive orders. The discussion below provides examples of some of the financial sanctions authorized by these laws and executive orders from 2010 through 2012.[20] According to an Under Secretary of the Treasury, the new legislation that Congress has enacted has increased financial and economic pressure on Iran.

In 2010, Congress passed the Comprehensive Iran Sanctions, Accountability, and Divestment Act of 2010 (CISADA) to amend the Iran Sanctions Act of 1996[21] and to enhance U.S. diplomatic efforts with respect to Iran by expanding economic sanctions targeting Iran.[22] According to an Under Secretary of the Treasury, "CISADA set a new precedent" because "... [i]t gave the Secretary of the Treasury the authority for the first time to require U.S. banks to terminate correspondent banking relationships with foreign banks that knowingly

---

[19]Our description focuses mainly on those financial sanctions targeting Iran found in laws, regulations, or executive orders that either (1) block the property of designated entities, or (2) target a financial transaction as an action that can result in the prohibition of the opening or the prohibition or imposition of strict conditions on the maintenance of a correspondent or payable-through account in the United States by a foreign financial institution. We generally focus on Treasury's authorities to implement financial sanctions targeting Iran. However, we recognize that the authorities we discuss do not represent an exhaustive list of all such financial sanctions regarding Iran.

[20]Although the scope of our review of financial sanctions targeting Iran spans from 2010 through 2012, we note that on January 2, 2013, the President signed the Iran Freedom and Counter-Proliferation Act of 2012 into law as part of the National Defense Authorization Act for Fiscal Year 2013. Pub. L. No. 112-239, §§ 1241-1255. This act authorizes further sanctions targeting Iran including adding sanctions for foreign financial institutions that facilitate financial transactions on behalf of certain specially designated nationals.

[21]In the Iran Sanctions Act of 1996 (previously known as the Iran-Libya Sanctions Act of 1996, or ILSA) Congress declared that it is the policy of the United States to deny Iran the ability to support acts of international terrorism and to fund the development and acquisition of weapons of mass destruction and the means to deliver them by limiting the development of Iran's ability to explore for, extract, refine, or transport by pipeline its petroleum resources. Pub. L. No. 104-172, § 3. Under the Act, the President shall sanction parties that engage in a number of activities including knowingly making an investment of $20 million or more that directly and significantly contributes to the enhancement of Iran's ability to develop its petroleum resources.

[22]Pub. L. No. 111-195, 124 Stat. 1312.

engaged in significant transactions with designated Iranian banks." Among other actions, section 104(c) of CISADA required the Secretary of the Treasury to prescribe regulations to prohibit or impose strict conditions on the opening or maintaining in the United States of a correspondent account or a payable-through account by a foreign financial institution found to have knowingly engaged in certain activities or facilitating a significant transaction by entities such as Iran's Islamic Revolutionary Guard Corps (IRGC).[23] Furthermore, section 104(d) of CISADA required Treasury to "prescribe regulations to prohibit any person owned or controlled by a domestic financial institution from knowingly engaging in…transactions with or benefitting the [IRGC]," its agents, or its affiliates whose property or interests in property are blocked pursuant to the International Emergency Economic Powers Act (IEEPA).[24] This provision in CISADA also extends certain monetary penalties under IEEPA (50 U.S.C. § 1705(b)) to domestic financial institutions if a person owned or controlled by the domestic financial institution violates the regulations and if the domestic financial institution knew, or should have known, about the violation.[25]

National Defense Authorization Act for Fiscal Year 2012

In 2011, Congress enacted the National Defense Authorization Act for Fiscal Year 2012 (NDAA).[26] The act required the President to block the property and interests in property, which is subject to U.S. jurisdiction, of all Iranian financial institutions, including the Central Bank of Iran.[27] In addition, the act required the President to prohibit the opening, and prohibit or impose strict conditions on the maintenance, of a correspondent or payable-through account in the United States by a foreign financial institution found to have knowingly conducted or facilitated any significant financial transaction with the Central Bank of Iran or another designated Iranian financial institution.[28] This sanction

---

[23]Pub. L. No. 111-195, § 104(c) (codified as amended at 22 U.S.C. § 8513(c)). Although the law uses the term "Iran's Revolutionary Guard Corps," Treasury refers to the IRGC as the "Iran's Islamic Revolutionary Guard Corps."

[24]Pub. L. No. 111-195, § 104(d).

[25]Id.

[26]Pub. L. No. 112-81, 125 Stat. 1298 (2011).

[27]See Pub. L. No. 112-81, § 1245(c) (codified as amended at 22 U.S.C. § 8513a).

[28]Pub. L. No. 112-81, § 1245(d).

applies to foreign central banks, only insofar as the transactions are related to the sale or purchase of petroleum or petroleum products to or from Iran.[29] Moreover, the sanction applied to transactions related to the purchase of petroleum or petroleum products from Iran only if the President has made a determination that there is a sufficient supply of petroleum or petroleum products from countries other than Iran.[30] However, if the President does determine that there is a sufficient supply of petroleum and petroleum products, the financial sanctions will not apply if the President determines that the country with primary jurisdiction over the foreign financial institution has significantly reduced its volume of crude oil purchases from Iran in a specific period.[31] The President delegated the authority to determine whether a country has significantly reduced the volume of Iranian crude oil purchases in a specific period to the Secretary of State, in consultation with the Secretary of the Treasury, the Secretary of Energy, and the Director of National Intelligence.[32]

Iran Threat Reduction and Syria Human Rights Act of 2012

In 2012, Congress passed the Iran Threat Reduction and Syria Human Rights Act of 2012 (TRA) to strengthen Iran sanctions laws for the purpose of compelling Iran to abandon its pursuit of nuclear weapons and other threatening activities and for other purposes.[33] TRA expanded sanctions in a number of areas including sanctions relating to Iran's energy sector.[34] For example, the TRA amends CISADA by requiring the Secretary of the Treasury to revise the regulations prescribed under CISADA section 104(c) to apply, to the same extent that they apply to a foreign financial institution found to knowingly engage in an activity described in CISADA section 104(c)(2), to a foreign financial institution

---

[29]Pub. L. No. 112-81, § 1245(d)(3). This restriction only applies to transactions that were conducted or facilitated on or after June 28, 2012. As originally enacted, this restriction applied to foreign financial institutions owned by a foreign government, including foreign central banks. The TRA later amended this restriction to apply only to foreign central banks. See Pub. L. No. 112-158, § 504.

[30]Pub. L. No. 112-81, § 1245(d)(4). Additionally, transactions involving exports of food, medicine or medical devices are excepted from the imposition of these sanctions. Pub. L. No. 112-81, § 1245(d)(2).

[31]Pub. L. No. 112-81 § 1245(d)(4)(D).

[32]Exec. Order No. 13599, § 11.

[33]Pub. L. No. 112-158, 126 Stat. 1214.

[34]Pub. L. No. 112-158, Title II.

that the Secretary of the Treasury finds (1) knowingly facilitates, or participates or assists in, an activity described in section 104(c)(2) of CISADA; (2) attempts or conspires to facilitate or participate in such an activity; or (3) is owned or controlled by a foreign financial institution that the Secretary finds knowingly engages in such an activity.[35] Moreover, section 312 of the TRA also amended CISADA to require Treasury to determine whether the National Iranian Oil Company or the National Iranian Tanker Company is an agent or affiliate of the IRGC.[36] On September 24, 2012, Treasury made a determination that the National Iranian Oil Company is an agent or affiliate of the IRGC.[37] Although the National Iranian Oil Company was already subject to sanctions under Executive Order 13599 (see below), according to Treasury, the determination that the National Iranian Oil Company is an agent or affiliate of the IRGC carries additional consequences. According to Treasury, as a result of the TRA section 312 determination, the National Iranian Oil Company is now an agent or affiliate of the IRGC, as described by CISADA section 104(c), whose property or interests in property are blocked pursuant to IEEPA. Furthermore, foreign financial institutions determined to have knowingly facilitated a significant transaction for the National Iranian Oil Company could have prohibitions or the imposition of strict conditions placed on their opening or maintenance of correspondent or payable-through accounts in the United States.[38]

Executive Orders under IEEPA

IEEPA granted the President a number of authorities, including the blocking of a foreign country's or foreign national's property, to respond to any unusual and extraordinary threat to the national security, foreign policy, or economy of the United States.[39] Administrations have invoked authority provided by IEEPA, as well as other authorities, to issue

---

[35]See Pub. L. No. 112-158, § 216.

[36]Pub. L. No. 112-158, § 312 (amending section CISADA section 104(c)). Treasury was required to make this determination by September 24, 2012.

[37]Although the law uses the term "Iran's Revolutionary Guard Corps," Treasury refers to the IRGC as the "Iran's Islamic Revolutionary Guard Corps."

[38]22 U.S.C. § 8513(c).

[39]50 U.S.C. §§ 1701 -1706.

executive orders that provide for sanctions targeting Iran.[40] The executive orders have imposed a number of sanctions, including a comprehensive trade and investment ban on Iran, and have been used to freeze the assets of parties designated for their engagement in proliferation or terrorism-related activities involving Iran.[41] Recently, the Obama administration has issued the following executive orders for additional steps to increase the sanctions on financial transactions relating to Iran:

- *Executive Order 13599 (February 5, 2012).*[42] This executive order blocked the property, and interests in property, of the government of Iran, and any Iranian financial institutions, including the Central Bank of Iran, that are in the United States. According to the executive order, this was done "in light of the deceptive practices of the Central Bank of Iran and other Iranian banks to conceal transactions of sanctioned parties, the deficiencies in Iran's anti-money laundering regime and the weaknesses in its implementation, and the continuing and unacceptable risk posed to the international financial system by Iran's activities." As a result of this blocking, no property of the government of Iran that is under the jurisdiction of the United States can be transferred, paid, exported, withdrawn, or otherwise dealt in.

- *Executive Order 13608 (May 1, 2012).*[43] This executive order authorized sanctions on a foreign person who has been determined to have facilitated deceptive transactions for or on behalf of any person subject to U.S. sanctions concerning Iran or Syria. The order defined, "deceptive transaction" as any transaction where the identity of any person subject to United States sanctions concerning Iran or Syria is

---

[40]For examples, see Exec. Order No. 12170, 44 Fed. Reg. 65729 (Nov. 14, 1979); Exec. Order No. 12957, 60 Fed. Reg. 14615 (Mar. 15, 1995); and Exec. Order No. 13059, 62 Fed. Reg. 44531 (Aug. 19, 1997).

[41]For example, Exec. Order No. 13059 (clarifying Executive Orders 12957 and 12959 and confirming that virtually all trade and investment activities with Iran by U.S. persons, wherever located, are prohibited). Under authorities granted in Executive Orders 13224 and 13382, Treasury has designated parties that engage in proliferation or terrorism-related activities involving Iran as subject to financial sanctions that freeze their assets and reduce their access to the U.S. financial system. Exec. Order No. 13224, 66 Fed. Reg. 49079 (Sept. 23, 2001) and Exec. Order No. 13382, 70 Fed. Reg. 38567 (June 28, 2005).

[42]77 Fed. Reg. 6659 (Feb. 8, 2012).

[43]77 Fed. Reg. 26409 (May 3, 2012).

withheld or obscured from other participants in the transaction or any relevant regulatory authorities.[44] Pursuant to the executive order, Treasury may prohibit all transactions or dealings, whether direct or indirect, involving a foreign person that it has determined to have facilitated deceptive transactions for, or on behalf of, any person subject to the requisite U.S. sanctions. According to Treasury, "[w]ith this new authority, Treasury now has the capability to publicly identify foreign individuals and entities that have engaged in these evasive and deceptive activities, and generally bar access to the U.S. financial and commercial systems."

- *Executive Order 13622 (July 30, 2012).*[45] This executive order authorized three new sanctions to be implemented by Treasury. First, the executive order authorized new sanctions on foreign financial institutions determined to have knowingly conducted or facilitated specified significant financial transactions with the National Iranian Oil Company or Naftiran Intertrade Company.[46] Second, the executive order authorized sanctions against foreign financial institutions found to have knowingly conducted or facilitated significant transactions for the purchase or acquisition of petroleum, petroleum products, or petrochemical products from Iran. Under the executive order, foreign financial institutions that engage in the two aforementioned activities could be prohibited from opening or maintaining correspondent or payable-through accounts in the United States.[47] Third, the executive order authorized Treasury to block the property of any person determined to have materially assisted, sponsored, or provided financial, material, or technological support for, or goods or services in support of, (1) the National Iranian Oil Company, the Naftiran Intertrade Company, or Central Bank of Iran or (2) the purchase or

---

[44]Exec. Order No. 13608, § 7.

[45]77 Fed. Reg. 45897 (Aug. 2, 2012).

[46]Exec. Order No. 13622, § 1(a). The sanctions shall not apply with respect to sales of refined petroleum products to the National Iranian Oil Company or to the Naftiran Intertrade Company that are below a certain dollar threshold.

[47]Exec. Order No. 13622, § 1(b). Sanctions regarding signification transactions with the National Iranian Oil Company or the Naftiran Intertrade Company or for the purchase or acquisition of petroleum or petroleum products shall not apply with respect to transactions for the sale of agricultural commodities, food, medicine, or medical devices when the underlying transaction has been authorized by Treasury. Exec. Order No. 13622, § 1(d), as amended by Exec. Order 13628.

acquisition of U.S. bank notes or precious metals by the government of Iran.[48] According to the executive order, these actions were taken "in light of the government of Iran's use of revenues from petroleum, petroleum products, and petrochemicals for illicit purposes; Iran's continued attempts to evade international sanctions through deceptive practices; and the unacceptable risk posed to the international financial system by Iran's activities."

- *Executive Order 13628 (October 9, 2012)*.[49] This executive order, among other things, blocked a person's property and interests in property in the United States or under the possession or control of a U.S. person once Treasury, in consultation with State, determines that the person has engaged in certain specified conduct.[50] For example, the executive order blocked the property of a person determined to have knowingly transferred or facilitated the transfer of goods, or technologies to Iran or any Iranian entity for use by the government of Iran to commit serious human rights abuses against the people of Iran. The executive order also prohibited any entity that is owned or controlled by a U.S. person and established outside the United States from knowingly engaging in any transaction with the Iranian government if that transaction would be prohibited under specified executive orders if it were engaged in by a U.S. person or in the United States.[51]

---

[48]Exec. Order No. 13622, § 5.

[49]77 Fed. Reg. 62139 (Oct. 12, 2012).

[50]Exec. Order No. 13628, §§ 2-3.

[51]Exec. Order No. 13628, § 4.

U.S. Agencies Administer and Enforce U.S. Financial Sanctions Targeting Iran

U.S. government agencies and regulators administer and enforce U.S. financial sanctions targeting Iran with banks' assistance. Treasury has primary responsibility for administering financial sanctions. State administers some investment and trade sanctions, principally energy sanctions, targeting Iran. Banks play an important role in the sanctions process by blocking transactions that are required to be blocked by U.S. law and reporting apparent violations to Treasury.[52] The federal and state banking regulators ensure effective compliance with these sanctions programs by the banks that they regulate. Treasury and other U.S. agencies have enforced sanctions through a variety of actions including issuing enforcement actions against entities that violate the sanctions. Specifically, since 2005, Treasury and Justice, in coordination with State and federal regulators, have taken actions against banks, assessing large financial settlements for systematic and willful violations of sanctions laws, including violations of Iran financial sanctions regulations. Table 1 lists the various U.S. entities involved in the administration and enforcement of U.S. financial sanctions targeting Iran, along with their respective roles and responsibilities.

---

[52]For the purposes of this report, we use the term "bank" to refer to an agent, agency, branch, or office within the United States of commercial banks, savings and loan associations, thrift institutions, credit unions, and foreign banks supervised by federal and or state banking regulators. For the purposes of the report, we use the term "apparent violations" to refer to apparent violations of OFAC sanctions regulations.

Table 1: U.S. Entities Involved in the Administration and Enforcement of Recent U.S. Financial Sanctions Targeting Iran

Administration of Sanctions	
Entities	**Roles and responsibilities**
Department of the Treasury	Develop and publish regulations to administer legislation and executive orders authorizing Treasury to administer financial sanctions. Conduct outreach with foreign governments and financial institutions. Analyze banking and financial information to identify the impact of the sanctions.
Department of State	Administer and enforce some investment and trade sanctions targeting Iran, principally energy sanctions targeting Iran. Is authorized to grant certain exceptions for countries reducing the volume of Iranian crude oil purchases.
Banks	Report blocked transactions to the Office of Foreign Assets Control (OFAC). Establish OFAC compliance programs. May report apparent violations to Treasury.
Federal and state banking regulators	Provide guidance on and examine banks' OFAC compliance programs.
Enforcement of Sanctions	
Entities	**Roles and responsibilities**
Department of the Treasury	Designate entities, impose sanctions, and apply enforcement actions for violations of financial sanctions laws and regulations.
Department of Justice	Pursue cases against persons, banks, and other financial institutions for criminal violations of financial sanctions laws and regulations.
Federal and state banking regulators	Issue enforcement actions related to OFAC compliance.

Source: GAO analysis of U.S. government agency documents.

Treasury, with State and Regulators, Is Responsible for Administering Financial Sanctions, with Assistance from Banks

Treasury has primary responsibility for administering the finance-related provisions of recent U.S. sanctions authorities by developing regulations, conducting outreach to domestic and foreign financial regulators and financial institutions, and identifying apparent sanctions violations. Treasury also assesses the effects of financial sanctions on the Iranian economy.

Regulations. OFAC developed and issued the Iranian Financial Sanctions Regulations to administer the financial sanctions enacted in July 2010

Three Treasury offices and one bureau are involved in administering the financial sanctions against Iran:

- The Office of Foreign Assets Control (OFAC) issues financial sanctions regulations, identifies apparent violations, conducts outreach to banks, designates entities connected with sanctions, and issues penalties for sanctions violations. OFAC is responsible for the administration of financial sanctions.

- The Office of Terrorist Financing and Financial Crimes assists in developing strategies for combating illicit financial transactions that support terrorist activity and weapons of mass destruction, which includes Iran. The Office of Terrorist Financing and Financial Crimes also conducts outreach with foreign governments and analyzes banking and financial information to identify the impact of the sanctions.

- The Financial Crimes Enforcement Network gathers information from banks to comply with CISADA section 104 (e), which requires banks to report on certain foreign correspondent bank accounts and transactions.

- The Office of Intelligence Analysis gathers all sources of information to analyze the impact of sanctions targeting Iran.

pursuant to CISADA.[53] Treasury has amended the Iranian Financial Sanctions Regulations to implement additional legislation, such as Section 1245 of NDAA.[54] While drafting, and before publishing regulations, OFAC solicited input on the proposed regulations from other Treasury officials and State. All U.S. persons must comply with the OFAC regulations, including all U.S. citizens, all persons and entities within the United States, and all U.S.-incorporated entities and their foreign branches.

Outreach. According to Treasury, since 2010, Treasury officials have conducted outreach to more than 145 foreign financial institutions in more than 60 countries as well as to foreign governments, regulators, and other trade groups and associations. U.S. embassy consulate staff in Dubai informed us that Treasury officials made several trips to the United Arab Emirates to conduct outreach with financial institutions. Financial officials we met with in Dubai confirmed that Treasury had provided them with information on the new sanctions regulations under CISADA. According to Treasury officials, Treasury conducted this outreach to raise awareness of U.S. financial sanctions.

Identification of violations. According to Treasury, OFAC continually compiles evidence and reviews information regarding potential sanctions violations from a variety of sources, including intelligence and public sources. Treasury officials stated that OFAC identifies potential violations through a variety of means, including financial irregularities from bank reports, referrals from federal bank regulators, and self-disclosures of potential violations by banks.[55] According to Treasury officials, when OFAC designates an entity because of its engagement in sanctionable

---

[53]Iranian Financial Sanctions Regulations, 75 Fed. Reg. 49836 (Aug. 16, 2010) (codified as amended at 31 C.F.R. pt. 561).

[54]Iranian Financial Sanctions Regulations, 77 Fed. Reg. 11724 (Feb. 27, 2012) (amending and reissuing the Iranian Financial Sanctions Regulations in their entirety).

[55]Federal banking regulators, as well as many state banking regulators, have entered into a Memorandum of Understanding with OFAC to facilitate the exchange of information between the regulators and OFAC. For example, officials from the Board of Governors of the Federal Reserve indicated that the agreement provides that the agency will notify OFAC when it is determined that there are "significant deficiencies" in a bank's OFAC compliance program, as well as notify OFAC of any specific violations of OFAC sanctions regulations that are found during the review of a bank's OFAC compliance program.

activity, OFAC declassifies and uses a portion of the evidence in order to make the designation public.

Assessments. Treasury regularly assesses the administration of sanctions and their impact on Iran. According to Treasury officials, Treasury gathers various sources of information to monitor and assess the impact of U.S. sanctions targeting Iran. Treasury officials indicated that they rely on Iranian press reports, input from banks and other financial institutions, Iranian economic indicators, and intelligence information, among other sources. According to U.S. consulate officers in Dubai, they monitor Iranian events and the Iranian economy, collecting information on trade, real estate, gold, and the volume of transactions in exchange houses in Iran. Treasury develops classified quarterly reports on the impacts of sanctions on Iran's economy, trade, and other sectors.

State

State is responsible for administering the significant reduction exception set forth in section 1245 of the NDAA of 2012.[56] The act requires the President to prohibit the opening, and prohibit or impose strict conditions on the maintenance, of a correspondent or payable-through account in the United States by a foreign financial institution found to have knowingly conducted or facilitated any significant financial transaction with the Central Bank of Iran or another designated Iranian financial institution.[57] The sanction applies to foreign central banks only insofar as the transactions are related to the sale or purchase of petroleum or petroleum products to or from Iran.[58] The sanction applies to transactions related to the purchase of petroleum or petroleum products from Iran only if the President has made a determination that there is a sufficient supply of petroleum or petroleum products from countries other than Iran. However, if the President does determine that there is a sufficient supply of petroleum and petroleum products, the financial sanctions will not apply if the President determines that the country with primary jurisdiction over the foreign financial institution has significantly reduced its volume of

---

[56] Pub. L. No. 112-81, § 1245(d)(4).

[57] Pub. L. No. 112-81, § 1245(d).

[58] Pub. L. No. 112-81, § 1245(d)(3). This restriction only applies to transactions that were conducted or facilitated on or after June 28, 2012.

crude oil purchases from Iran in a specific period.[59] The President delegated the authority to determine whether a country has significantly reduced the volume of Iranian crude oil purchases in a specific period to the Secretary of State, in consultation with the Secretary of the Treasury, the Secretary of Energy, and the Director of National Intelligence.[60] The Secretary of State's determinations are based on an assessment of each country's efforts to reduce the volume of crude oil imported from Iran. According to State, the Secretary of State considers various factors, including the quantity and percentage of the reduction in purchases of Iranian crude oil over the relevant period; termination of contracts for future delivery of Iranian crude oil; and other actions that demonstrate a commitment to substantially decrease such purchases. On the basis of the assessment led by State, the Secretary of State granted exceptions to 20 countries, including China, Japan, the Republic of Korea, and India, for "significantly" reducing their volume of crude oil purchases from Iran since the enactment of the NDAA.[61]

Banks

According to American Bankers Association and Institute of International Bankers officials, banks' sanctions compliance efforts include the use of software screening tools to avoid conducting transactions with sanctioned entities. In addition to reporting, federal guidance states that banks should establish OFAC compliance programs as a matter of sound banking practice and to ensure compliance with regulations. In general, federal banking regulators expect each bank to establish and maintain an effective, written OFAC compliance program commensurate with its OFAC risk profile. According to the regulators' guidance, banks' compliance programs should

- identify high-risk areas,
- provide for appropriate internal controls for screening and reporting,
- establish independent testing for compliance, designate bank a staff responsible for OFAC compliance, and
- create training programs for appropriate personnel in all relevant areas of the bank.

The guidance also identified the bank's assessment of its specific product lines, customer base, and nature of transactions and identification of higher-risk areas for OFAC transactions as a fundamental element of a sound OFAC compliance program.

Banks play an important role in the sanctions process by blocking property or interests in property that are required to be blocked under U.S. law and by reporting apparent violations to Treasury. Iran sanctions regulations generally require banks to block transactions that (1) are by, or on behalf of, a blocked individual or entity; (2) are to, or go through, a blocked entity; or (3) are in connection with a transaction in which a blocked individual or entity has an interest.[62] Banks holding, receiving, or

---

[59]Pub. L. No. 112-81 § 1245(d)(4)(D), codified as amended at 22 U.S.C. § 8513a. Effective February 6, 2013 section 504 of the Iran Threat Reduction and Syria Human Rights Act of 2012 amended the significant reduction exception. The modifications do not impact this report's discussion of the exception. See Pub. L. No. 112-158, § 504 for the full amendment.

[60]Exec. Order No. 13599, § 11.

[61]Between March 2012 and December 2012, the Secretary of State granted exceptions to 20 countries–Belgium, China, Czech Republic, France, Germany, Greece, India, Italy, Japan, Malaysia, the Netherlands, Poland, Republic of Korea, Singapore, South Africa, Spain, Sri Lanka, Turkey, Taiwan, and the United Kingdom–for reductions in the volume of their crude oil purchases from Iran.

[62]31 C.F.R. § 560.211. OFAC defines blocking or "freezing" as a form of controlling assets under U.S. jurisdiction. According to OFAC, while the title to blocked property remains with the designated country or national, the exercise of the powers and privileges normally associated with ownership is prohibited without authorization from OFAC. OFAC also states that blocking immediately imposes an across-the-board prohibition against transfers or transactions of any kind with regard to the property.

blocking transfers of blocked property must report to OFAC within 10 days of the property becoming blocked.[63] Banks must place the assets or funds in a segregated interest-bearing account.[64]

In addition, banks may report apparent violations to Treasury. Treasury officials stated that once a bank discloses an apparent sanctions violation to Treasury, the bank often engages in a thorough review of its own past conduct and provides information to OFAC. According to OFAC officials, the bank generally presents an overview of its transactions and the context in which they occurred, and OFAC provides direction on where additional review is needed from the banks. After the disclosure, OFAC asks the bank to identify other recipients of the information of the transactions. After OFAC's review, OFAC then makes a determination on the possibility of enforcement. The civil penalty for violating the Iran financial sanctions regulations may be as much as $250,000 per violation or twice the amount of the transaction, whichever is greater.[65]

Multiple U.S. Agencies Enforce Financial Sanctions

Treasury Has Designated Entities, Imposed Sanctions, and Applied Enforcement Actions for Violations of Financial Sanctions

Designating entities. As part of its enforcement efforts, Treasury has used a range of actions to enforce sanctions targeting Iran, including designating entities for engaging in sanctionable activity related to Iran, imposing sanctions on financial institutions, and issuing enforcement actions against financial entities. For example, according to Treasury, OFAC publishes a list of individuals and entities that have been designated for engaging in certain conduct, as well as a list of individuals and entities owned or controlled by, or acting for or on behalf of those previously listed individuals and entities. OFAC also identifies individuals and entities that are officials of; are owned or controlled by; or act on

---

[63]31 C.F.R. § 501.603.

[64]31 C.F.R. § 560.213.

[65]31 C.F.R. §§ 560.701 and 561.701.

behalf of certain countries.[66] OFAC blocks the assets of these entities and individuals and generally prohibits U.S. persons from dealing with them. According to Treasury, as of January 2013, OFAC had designated more than 360 individuals and entities–including banks, energy companies, and businesses–linked to Iran's weapons-of-mass-destruction program and support for terrorism under various Iran-related executive orders. These designations included actions taken under Treasury's executive order authorities related to the proliferation of weapons of mass destruction or delivery systems for weapons of mass destruction and international terrorism.[67]

Imposing sanctions. In July 2012, Treasury imposed sanctions under CISADA on two foreign financial institutions—the Bank of Kunlun (China) and Elaf Islamic Bank (Iraq)—for knowingly facilitating significant transactions and providing significant financial services for designated Iranian banks. According to Treasury documents, the action against the two banks effectively barred the banks from directly accessing the U.S. financial system. In addition, financial institutions may not open correspondent or payable-through accounts for Bank of Kunlun or Elaf Islamic Bank in the United States, and any financial institutions that held such accounts were required to close them within 10 days of the imposition of the sanction.

Applying enforcement actions. OFAC has also issued enforcement actions against banks for violations or apparent violations of Iran sanctions regulations. From 2005 through 2012, OFAC imposed 45 civil penalties against banks for facilitating transactions in apparent violation of Iran sanctions regulations.[68] The penalty and settlement amounts for apparent violations varied significantly. For example, in May 2006 OFAC announced a settlement with a bank for $3,352 in connection with an unauthorized funds transfer involving Iran. In June 2012, OFAC

---

[66]As part of its enforcement efforts, OFAC publishes a list of individuals and companies owned or controlled by, or acting for or on behalf of, targeted countries. It also lists individuals, groups, and entities, such as terrorists and narcotics traffickers designated under programs that are not country-specific. Collectively, such individuals and companies are called "Specially Designated Nationals" or "SDNs."

[67]Exec. Order No. 13224 and Exec. Order No. 13822.

[68]OFAC published its enforcement procedures for banks because banks play a unique role in implementing OFAC sanctions programs and because of the nature of the transactions in which banks engage.

announced a $619 million settlement with ING Direct Bank N.V. to address, in part, apparent violations of the Iranian Transaction Regulations, among other sanctions programs, over a number of years and involving a total of $1.6 billion in transactions. All enforcement actions published to date involve violations of Iran sanctions regulations that were enacted before 2007.

Federal and State Banking Regulators, with OFAC, Have Imposed Enforcement Actions

Federal and state banking regulators have imposed enforcement actions concurrently, or in close coordination, with OFAC in cases of significant failures to comply with OFAC regulations. For example, in 2005 the Federal Reserve, FinCEN, the New York State Banking Department, the Illinois Department of Financial and Professional Regulation, and OFAC announced the assessment of penalties against the Dutch bank ABN AMRO based, in part, on OFAC violations.[69] The agencies jointly assessed $75 million in penalties against the bank on the basis of findings that it participated in transactions that violated U.S. sanctions laws, as well as findings of the bank's failures related to U.S. anti-money laundering laws and regulations and other banking laws.[70]

In a recent case, federal and state banking regulators did not impose enforcement actions at the same time. In August 2012, the New York State Department of Financial Services announced that Standard Chartered Bank had agreed to a settlement of $340 million and the implementation of remedial actions in connection with the omission of Iranian customer information from U.S. dollar payment messages sent to U.S. financial institutions with respect to 59,000 transactions that totaled approximately $250 billion. The regulator determined that the bank's policies and procedures during the relevant period prevented examiners

---

[69]In October 2007, a consortium of banks led by the Royal Bank of Scotland Group PLC acquired ABN AMRO. In October 2011, the State of New York abolished the New York State Banking Department and the New York State Insurance Department, and their authorities transferred to the New York State Department of Financial Services.

[70]ABN AMRO also volunteered to pay $5 million to the Illinois Bank Examiners' Education Foundation. The Board of Governors of the Federal Reserve System, the New York State Banking Department, and the Illinois Department of Financial and Professional Regulation announced the issuance, together with De Nederlandsche Bank N.V (the regulator of Dutch banks) of a Consent Cease and Desist Order against ABN AMRO and its branches in New York, New York and Chicago, Illinois. The order incorporated and largely superseded a 2004 written agreement among ABN AMRO, its New York Branch, the Federal Reserve Bank of New York, the Federal Reserve Bank of Chicago, the New York State Banking Department, and the Illinois Department of Financial and Professional Regulation.

from performing complete safety and soundness examinations, and from identifying suspicious patterns of activity that could, among other things, allow regulators to assist law enforcement authorities. In December 2012, OFAC announced a settlement with Standard Chartered for $132 million for apparent violations of U.S. sanctions laws and regulations. In a separate action, also in December 2012, the Federal Reserve also imposed a $100 million civil money penalty against the bank and its New York branch, a portion of which related to unsafe and unsound banking practices associated with the insufficient oversight of its compliance program for U.S. sanctions.

Justice Has Pursued Cases against Banks for Violations of Financial Sanctions Laws

From 2009 to 2012, Justice, through its Criminal Division, National Security Division, and U.S. Attorney's Offices, pursued criminal investigations against seven banks for potential violations of sanctions laws that involved transactions with Iran. All seven cases involved banks' potential violations of IEEPA, under which it is criminal to violate, or attempt to violate, regulations issued under those statutes. Criminal investigations against banks for sanctions violations were resolved through settlements that involved monetary forfeitures and deferred prosecution agreements (see table 2).[71]

Table 2: Banks against Which the Department of Justice Has Pursued Charges for Transactions with Sanctioned Entities, Including Iran, 2009-2012

Year	Bank	Forfeiture Amount
2012	HSBC Bank USA N.A.	$1.256 billion[a]
2012	Standard Chartered Bank	$227 million[b]
2012	ING Bank N.V.	$619 million[c]
2010	Barclays Bank PLC	$298 million[d]
2010	ABN AMRO Bank N.V.	$500 million
2009	Credit Suisse AG	$536 million[e]
2009	Lloyds TSB Bank PLC	$350 million[f]

Source: GAO analysis of court documents.

[71]Deferred prosecution agreements between Justice and banks have involved agreement by prosecutors to defer prosecution of the banks for a specified time and agreement by the banks to, among other things, admit publicly the facts of their misconduct, cooperate fully with prosecutors, and implement certain corrective actions.

Senior law enforcement officials cited threats to both national security and the integrity of the U.S. financial system posed by the banks' misconduct. Furthermore, in each investigation, the bank systematically removed or obscured payment data that would have revealed the involvement of sanctioned countries and entities, including Iran. For example, in 2009, Credit Suisse AG agreed to a one-count filing in federal court that charged the bank with violating IEEPA. Justice determined that from 1995 through 2006, Credit Suisse AG in European locations deliberately removed material information, such as customer names, bank names, and addresses, from payment messages so that the wire transfers would pass undetected through filters at U.S. banks. Credit Suisse AG also provided its Iranian clients with a pamphlet that provided detailed payment instructions on how to avoid triggering U.S. OFAC filters. The scheme allowed U.S.-sanctioned countries and entities to move hundreds of millions of dollars through the U.S. financial system.

In another investigation, Justice indicated that beginning in the early 1990s until 2007, ING Bank N.V. violated U.S. law by moving more than $2 billion illegally through the U.S. financial system–via more than 20,000 transactions–on behalf of entities subject to U.S. economic sanctions, including Cuba and Iran. According to Justice, bank staff intentionally manipulated financial and trade transactions to remove references to Iran and other sanctioned countries to avoid detection by software filters used by unaffiliated banks in the United States.[72]

Similarly, in December 2012, both HSBC Holdings, PLC and HSBC Bank USA N.A. entered into a deferred prosecution agreement with Justice for violations of IEEPA and the Trading With the Enemy Act in connection with Iran and other sanctioned countries.[73] Court documents indicated that from the mid-1990s through September 2006, HSBC Holdings, PLC allowed approximately $660 million in OFAC-prohibited transactions to be processed through U.S. financial institutions, including HSBC Bank USA N.A. According to an official from the Federal Reserve, HSBC Holdings, PLC permitted subsidiaries in Europe and the Middle East to follow instructions from sanctioned countries, including Iran, to omit and otherwise obscure their names from U.S. dollar payment messages sent to HSBC Bank USA N.A. and other financial institutions located in the United States.

According to a senior Justice official, prosecutors sought to obtain the appropriate dispositions of cases against banks for criminal violations of financial sanctions laws. Federal guidelines regarding prosecution of business organizations direct prosecutors to consider additional factors to those normally considered in prosecuting individuals. The guidelines direct federal prosecutors to consider factors including the timely and voluntary disclosure of the wrongdoing by the business and its willingness to cooperate in the investigation, among others. In announcing the deferred agreements, Justice officials cited the banks' remedial actions, willingness to accept responsibility, and significant cooperation during the investigations.

---

[72]ING Bank N.V.'s settlements with Justice and the New York County District Attorney's Office satisfied a settlement reached with OFAC.

[73]The $1.256 billion forfeiture and deferred prosecution agreement also addressed violations of the Bank Secrecy Act, involving approximately $881 million. The forfeiture to Justice satisfied a $375 million settlement with OFAC. HSBC Holdings, PLC. also agreed to pay $665 million in civil penalties—$500 million levied by the Office of the Comptroller of the Currency and $165 million by the Board of Governors of the Federal Reserve System—for anti-money laundering program violations. The Office of the Comptroller of the Currency penalty also satisfied a $500 million civil penalty for FinCEN. HSBC Group is a United Kingdom corporation that is headquartered in London. As of January 2013, the United Kingdom's Financial Services Authority was pursuing a separate action.

U.S. and International Sanctions Have Adversely Affected the Iranian Economy, and Iran Is Attempting to Adapt to Them

The combination of the various U.S. and international trade, investment, and financial sanctions has adversely affected the Iranian economy and its future outlook. Our analysis indicates that the Iranian economy has consistently underperformed comparable peer countries across key economic indicators since the enactment of U.S. and international sanctions between 2010 and 2012. Furthermore, professional and International Monetary Fund (IMF) forecasters revised their projections of the Iranian economy after the enactment of sanctions to reflect deterioration in its expected performance. U.S. and EU exports of humanitarian goods to Iran increased in the first three quarters of 2012 compared with 2011, according to our analysis of trade data. According to open source reports, the government of Iran is attempting to adapt to the sanctions through various means, including using alternative payment mechanisms such as barter agreements, but thus far these agreements have not fully offset Iran's reduced oil exports.

U.S. and International Sanctions Have Adversely Affected the Iranian Economy

U.S. and international sanctions have adversely affected the Iranian economy. Experts and U.S. officials have indicated that the sanctions have created a number of difficulties for the Iranian economy and that the financial sanctions have limited Iran's ability to conduct trade and finance. Following the enactment of sanctions beginning in 2010, Iran's oil production, oil export revenue, and gross domestic product (GDP) have declined relative to comparable countries, and inflation has increased. Moreover, IMF and professional forecasters downgraded their projections of Iranian economic performance to reflect a deterioration of the Iranian economy, specifically with regard to GDP, inflation, and unemployment, since the enactment of recent sanctions.

Sanctions Have Created a Number of Difficulties for the Iranian Economy

U.S. and international sanctions have created a number of difficulties for the Iranian economy. Some experts stated that the deterioration in Iran's recent economic performance resulted from a combination of sanctions—including U.S. and international sanctions—and economic mismanagement by the government of Iran. The recent sanctions are likely to have reduced Iran's ability to ship and sell oil, an important component of the economy and historically a key source of foreign currency earnings and government revenue. U.S. financial sanctions have made receiving payment for oil and other exports more difficult. U.S. officials and representatives from financial institutions said that U.S. financial sanctions have increasingly denied Iran access to U.S. and international financial institutions, limiting its ability to finance trade and conduct other financial transactions, and increasing transaction costs. For example, according to officials from some international financial institutions, many foreign banks are unwilling to process transactions for Iranian businesses and citizens even when it was not clear that these transactions would trigger sanctions. In addition, as already noted, in 2012 Iranian banks designated by the EU were cut off from the largest financial messaging service, SWIFT, which processed more than 2 million financial messages for 29 Iranian financial institutions in 2011.

The Iranian Economy Has Consistently Underperformed Peer Economies since 2010

To help isolate economic changes that are unique to Iran we identified a set of comparable countries (peers) to serve as benchmarks for Iranian economic performance. We identified 23 peers that were either countries in the same region as Iran or countries with a similar share of oil in their exports.[74] We used this combined peer group to assess the performance of Iran's oil market, GDP, and inflation.

Oil production. Iranian oil production sharply diverged from peer oil production beginning in 2011 (see fig. 2).

---

[74]The combined peer group allows us to isolate economic changes that are unique to Iran but does not necessarily identify the impact of sanctions. The peer group includes the IMF's Middle East and North Africa (MENA) region, neighbors not included in MENA, and oil export dependent countries outside the region. We excluded certain countries experiencing significant instability due to civil unrest or other conflict. The peer group comprises Algeria, Angola, Armenia, Azerbaijan, Bahrain, Djibouti, Egypt, Equatorial Guinea, Gabon, Jordan, Kuwait, Mauritania, Morocco, Oman, Panama, Republic of Congo, Qatar, Saudi Arabia, Tunisia, Turkey, Turkmenistan, United Arab Emirates, and Venezuela. For a complete description of our peer group selection and analysis, see appendix III.

Figure 2: Oil Production for Iran and Peers, January 2000 through June 2012

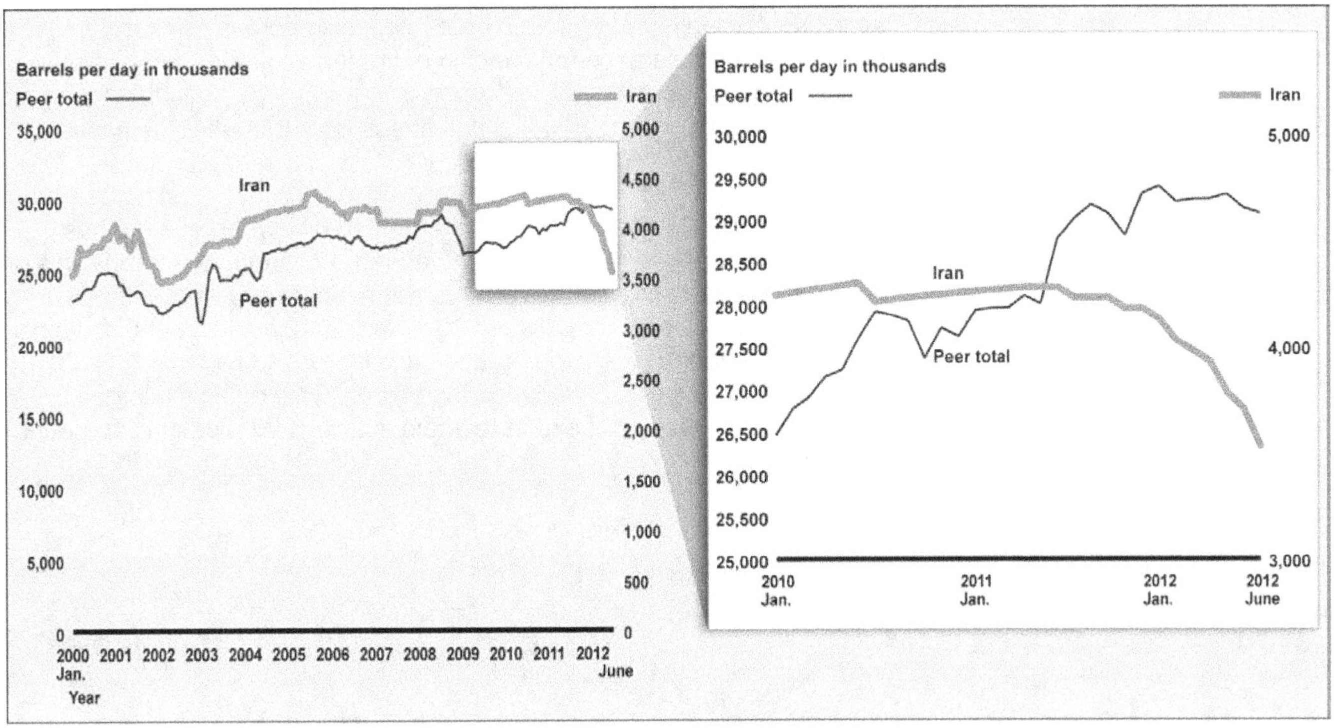

Source: GAO analysis of Energy Information Administration data

Note: The oil production shown for peers is based on the combined production of all peers.

Iranian oil production has fallen by more than 16 percent since July 2010, while production by peers concurrently increased by roughly 4 percent according to our analysis of data from the Energy Information Administration. However, significant deterioration in oil production and exports did not occur until 2012. According to our econometric analysis, oil production dropped by a statistically significant 26 percent more than expected (on an annualized basis) in 2012.[75] Several aspects of the sanctions have reduced Iran's ability to produce oil. U.S. officials and

---

[75]We controlled for historical trends in oil production in the Iranian economy as well as contemporaneous changes in peers' economies. Although this approach helps isolate economic changes that are unique to Iran, concurrent events such as economic policies in Iran imply that factors in addition to sanctions may be affecting its economy. See appendix III for more information about our econometric analysis.

independent experts stated that U.S. and international sanctions have limited foreign investment in Iran's oil and gas sectors. Furthermore, EU sanctions, including an embargo on Iranian oil imports as well as prohibitions on insurance for shipping of Iranian oil and petrochemicals, were adopted in January 2012.[76] According to State, 20 countries reduced their volume of crude oil purchases from Iran after the passage of NDAA.

Revenue from oil exports. Since 2010, Iranian oil export revenue has declined while peers' revenue has increased. According to our analysis of IMF data, Iranian oil export revenue is estimated to have declined by approximately 18 percent between 2010 and 2012, while peers' combined oil exports revenues are estimated to have increased by more than 50 percent over the same time period (see fig. 3). This reflects a large estimated decrease in oil export revenue in Iran in 2012 relative to peers.

---

[76]Council Decision 2012/35/CFSP.

Figure 3: Oil Export Revenue for Iran and Peers, 2000 through 2012

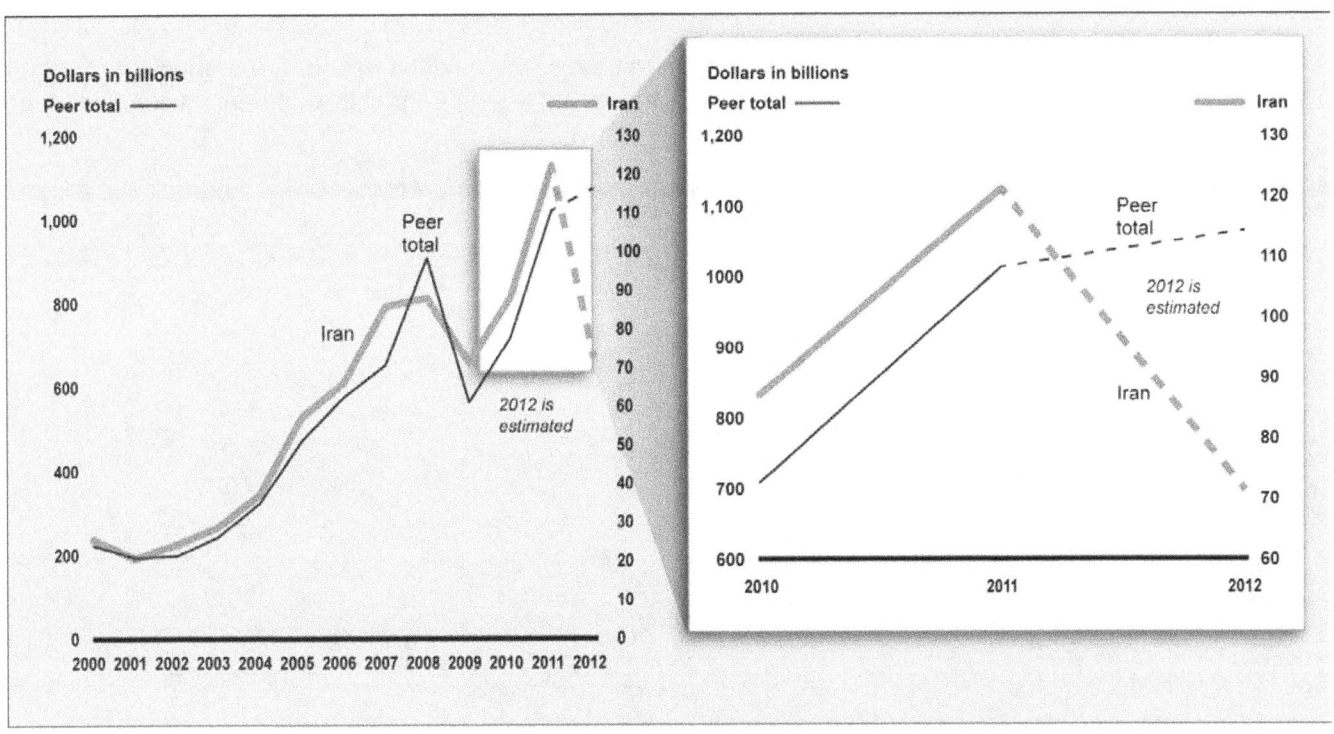

Source: GAO analysis of International Monetary Fund data.

Note: The export revenue shown for peers is based on the combined oil revenues for all peers.

According to open source reports, the International Energy Agency stated that Iranian oil exports declined from about 2.5 million barrels per day in 2011 to about 1.3 million barrels per day in November 2012.[77] Declining export revenue is principally driven by lower estimates of oil exports, but lower prices may also be a factor. According to one expert we spoke with, Iran may be offering as much as a 10 percent discount from its official selling price to some customers. Revenue from oil exports is an important component of government revenue in Iran and IMF estimates that Iran

[77]The International Energy Agency is an international organization composed of 28 member nations of the Organisation for Economic Co-operation and Development that, among other things, collects energy data and produces data on the supply, transformation, and consumption of major energy sources.

ran its largest budget deficit since 1998—almost 3 percent of GDP—in 2012.

GDP. GDP—an aggregate measure of an economy's production of goods and services—has increased less in Iran relative to peers since 2010 (see fig. 4).

Figure 4: GDP for Iran and Peers, January 2010 through July 2012

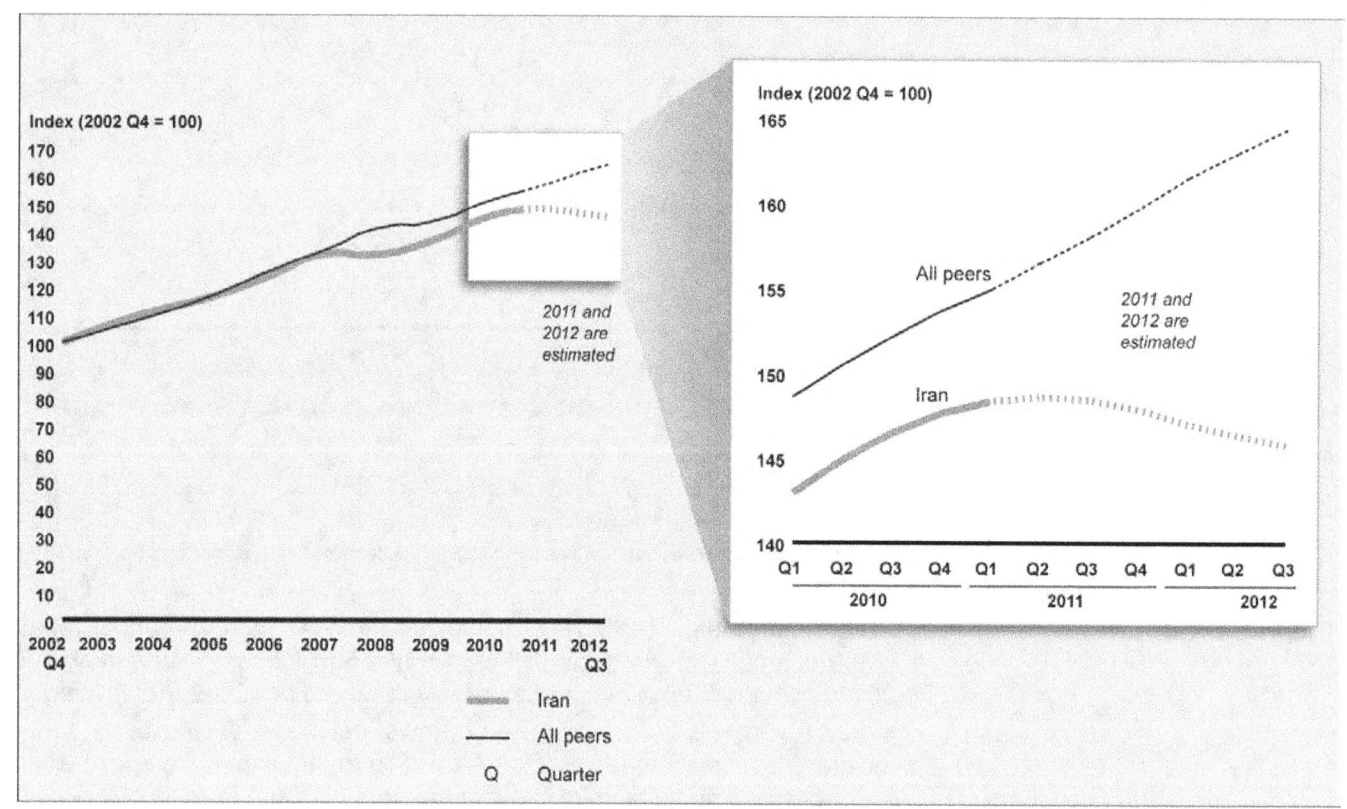

Source: GAO analysis of International Monetary Fund, IHS Global Insight, and Economist Intelligence Unit data.

Note: The GDP shown for peers is based on an index set to 100 in the fourth quarter of 2002. The index grows at the median growth rate of Iran's peers each quarter. For 2012 estimates, we adjusted quarterly GDP growth in Iran to be consistent with a consensus annual estimate based on the average of IMF, IHS Global Insight, and Economist Intelligence Unit annual estimates.

Because official estimates of GDP have not been available since 2010, we averaged estimates from IMF and two private economic information services. The resulting consensus estimates indicate that the Iranian economy grew by 1.9 percent in 2011 and shrank by 1.4 percent in 2012.

In contrast, Iran's median peer economy grew by 4.2 percent in both 2011 and 2012.[78]

Inflation. Annual inflation in Iran, which has historically been higher and more volatile than inflation in peer countries, increased from almost 8 percent in 2010 to 27 percent in late 2012, while median peer inflation remained lower, between 4 and 6 percent (see fig. 5).

Figure 5: Consumer Price Inflation for Iran and Peers, January 2005 through July 2012

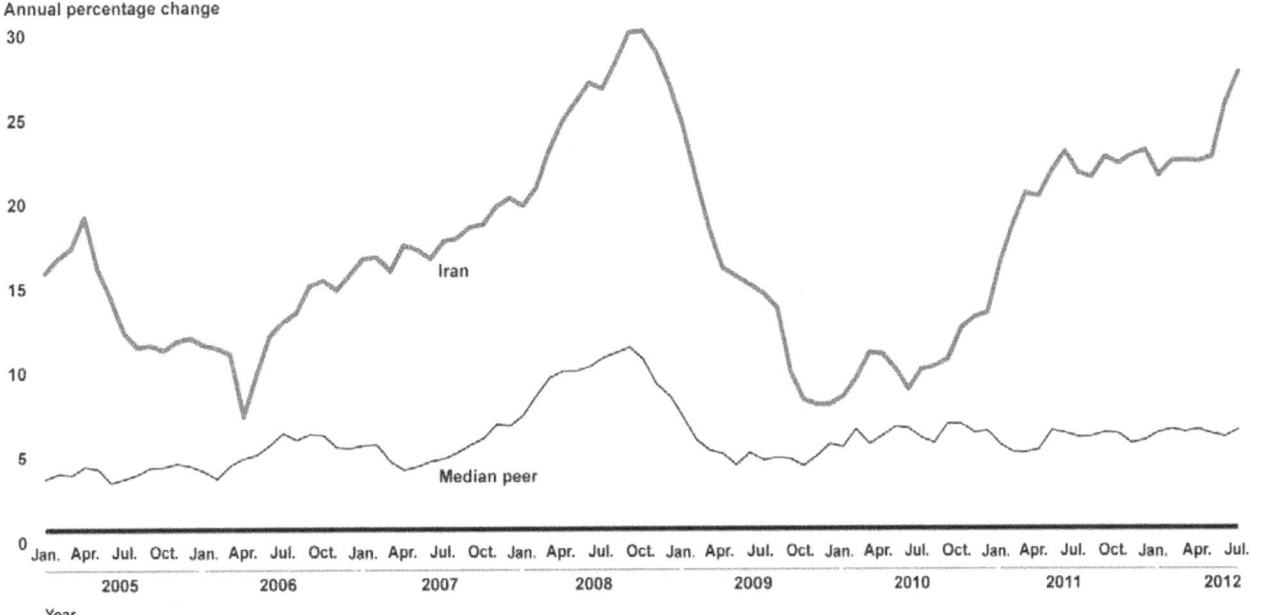

Source: GAO analysis of International Monetary Fund data.

Note: The inflation shown for peers is based on median annual (year-on-year) inflation for Iran's peers. We omitted certain countries because of a lack of available data at the time of our analysis. We obtained similar results when we calculated peer inflation using a simple average or an average weighted by peer GDP.

According to our econometric analysis, inflation increased by a statistically significant 12.6 percentage points more than expected (on an

---

[78]We obtained similar results when we calculated peer GDP growth using a simple average or an average weighted by peer GDP. We did not attempt to adjust for differences in fiscal-year and calendar-year reporting across Iran and its peers.

annualized basis) in 2012.[79] As recently as 2010, Iran had reduced inflation to below 10 percent, down from nearly 30 percent in 2008. Higher inflation may also have been driven in part by higher transaction costs resulting from U.S. financial sanctions that made processing payments for imports more costly. One measure of the Iranian rial-dollar market exchange rate depreciated almost 70 percent from July 2010 to October 2012. The depreciating exchange rate increased the price of certain imported goods, which also likely contributed to the increase in inflation.[80] In December 2010, the government of Iran introduced a reform of energy subsidies that increased energy prices and hence also had an impact on inflation. One expert has suggested that excessive money growth by the Central Bank of Iran also contributed to higher inflation.[81]

Forecasters Have Downgraded Projections for the Post-2012 Iranian Economy

Three forecasters—IHS Global Insight, IMF, and the Economist Intelligence Unit—have downgraded their forecasts of the Iranian economy to reflect a deterioration in Iran's expected economic performance after the enactment of recent U.S. and international sanctions. We compared the forecasts performed before and after the latest round of sanctions, and found that the forecasts predicted poorer performance on key macroeconomic indicators, such as Iranian GDP, inflation, and unemployment, between 2012 and 2016 than was previously expected. For example, according to IHS Global Insight, Iran will continue to face declining oil output, plunging exports, surging prices, and a sharply weaker currency after 2012.

Real GDP. Before recent sanctions were enacted from July 2010 through 2012, the three forecasters predicted that between 2012 and 2016, the Iranian economy would grow, on average, by about 3.2 to 4.3 percent per

---

[79]We controlled for historical inflation trends in the Iranian economy as well as contemporaneous changes in peers' economies. Although this approach helps to isolate economic changes that are unique to Iran, concurrent events such as economic policies in Iran imply that factors in addition to the sanctions may be affecting its economy. See appendix III for more information on the econometric analysis.

[80]If the desire to move savings out of Iran (capital flight) is driving the depreciation of the exchange rate, then the depreciation itself would cause inflation by making imports more expensive. However, in the absence of, or in addition to, capital flight, higher inflation could be driving the depreciation, given that the purchasing power of the rial has fallen.

[81]These policy responses may have been driven in part by the sanctions. For example, IHS Global Insight has argued that sanctions played a major role in the Iranian government's implementation of subsidy reform.

year. However, in their updates, published in October and November 2012, all three forecasters predicted that Iran's annual GDP would grow, on average, by -0.5 to 0.8 percent for the same period (see fig. 6).

Figure 6: Forecasts of Iran's GDP Before and After Recent U.S. and International Sanctions

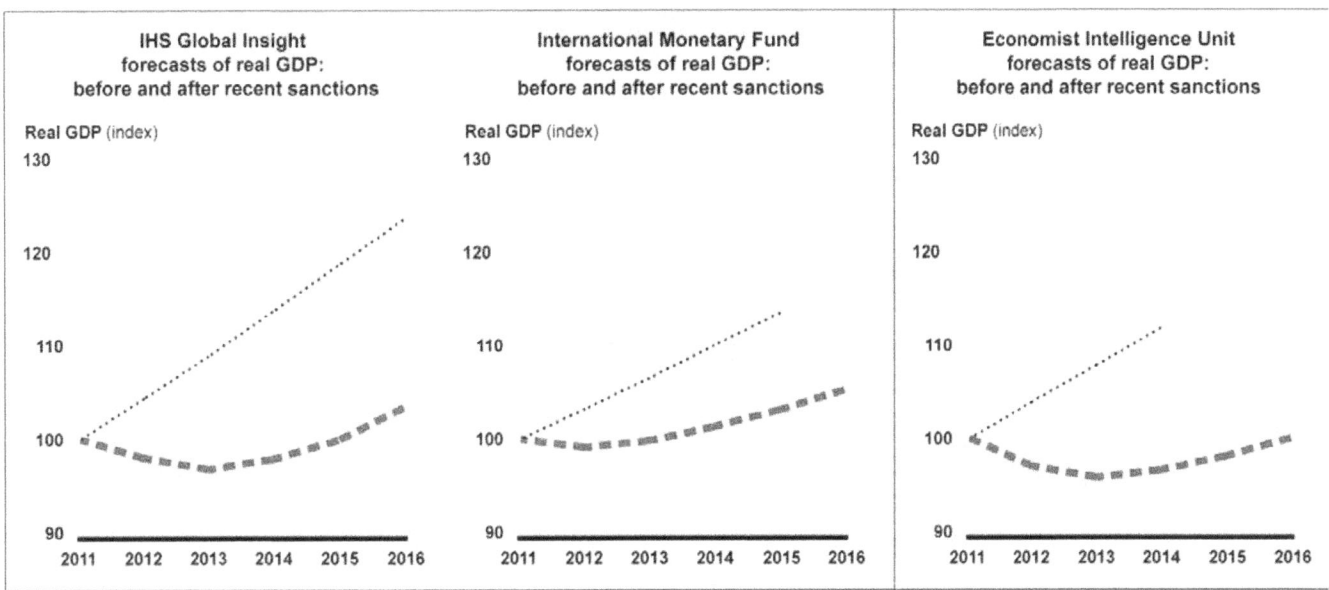

- - - - Before recent sanctions

▪ ▪ ▪ ▪ After recent sanctions

Source: GAO analysis of data from IHS Global Insight, the International Monetary Fund's World Economic Outlook, and the Economist Intelligence Unit.

According to IHS Global Insight, the U.S. and EU sanctions that target Iranian oil exports and the Central Bank of Iran are harsher and more punitive than previously enacted sanctions, and will likely push the Iranian economy into recession. In particular, after updating its forecast in August 2012, IHS Global Insight expected the Iranian economy to contract by 2.0 percent in 2012 and by 1.3 percent in 2013. According to the IMF's Regional Economic Outlook for the Middle East and Central Asia of November 2012, Iran's oil production has declined owing to tightened U.S. sanctions and the EU oil embargo, lowering the country's growth outlook. All three forecasters predicted that Iran's crude production and exports would continue their downward trend as a result of the sanctions and that Iran would be heavily reliant on its Asian and Middle Eastern trading partners to purchase crude oil available for exports. Furthermore, the IMF's Regional Economic Outlook projected that Iran's gross official reserves would decline from $101.5 billion in 2011 to $89.2 billion in 2012 and $84.6 billion in 2013. Based on the IMF's projections of Iran's annual imports of goods and services in 2012 and 2013, the anticipated reserves will be less than Iran's annual imports. Although the forecasters projected that the negative trend of real GDP would likely reverse in or after 2013, the Economist Intelligence Unit, for example, did not take into account any future changes in current sanctions or the possible enactment of new sanctions.

Inflation. The forecasters revised the projected inflation rate for Iran to reflect predicted future economic environment that was worse than originally projected (see fig. 7).

Figure 7: Forecasts of Iranian Inflation Before and After Recent U.S. and International Sanctions

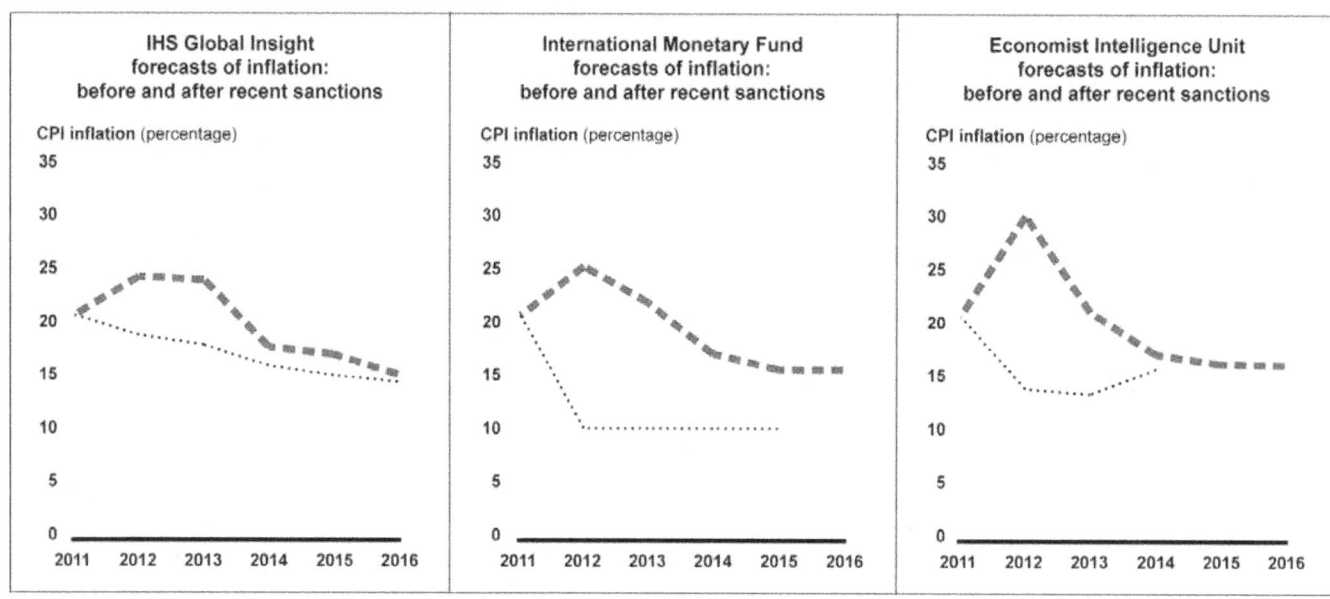

.... Before recent sanctions

▪ ▪ ▪ ▪ After recent sanctions

Source: GAO analysis of data from IHS Global Insight, the International Monetary Fund's World Economic Outlook, and the Economist Intelligence Unit.

Before recent sanctions were enacted, the average annual inflation rate predicted by IHS Global Insight, IMF, and the Economist Intelligence Unit ranged between 10.0 and 16.3 percent for the period from 2012 to 2016. However, the revised forecasts predicted that inflation would average 19.0 to 21.0 percent for the same period. According to the three forecasters, the near-term inflation outlook for Iran has deteriorated in light of subsidy cuts, the collapsing value of the Iranian rial, and additional EU and U.S. sanctions. For example, according to the Economic Intelligence Unit, inflation will remain high, driven by the removal of subsidies and by sanctions, which are leading to a dramatic weakening of the unofficial value of the rial and surging prices for imports. Since Iran is a major consumer of refined petroleum, a domestic production shortage means that the country needs to import refined petroleum to meet demand, exacerbating the vulnerability to import price inflation. Furthermore, the Economic Intelligence Unit anticipated that in the face of declining government revenue, there is a risk that the authorities will print money to fund spending, which could feed an inflationary spiral. IHS Global Insight projected higher inflation over the next 5 years to reflect the move to further reduce—and ultimately eliminate—potentially costly government subsidies on food, utilities, education, and other goods and services.

Unemployment. In addition to expecting the economy to shrink in the near term, the forecasters also revised their projections of the employment outlook for Iran (see fig. 8).

Figure 8: Forecasts of Iranian Unemployment Before and After Recent U.S. and International Sanctions

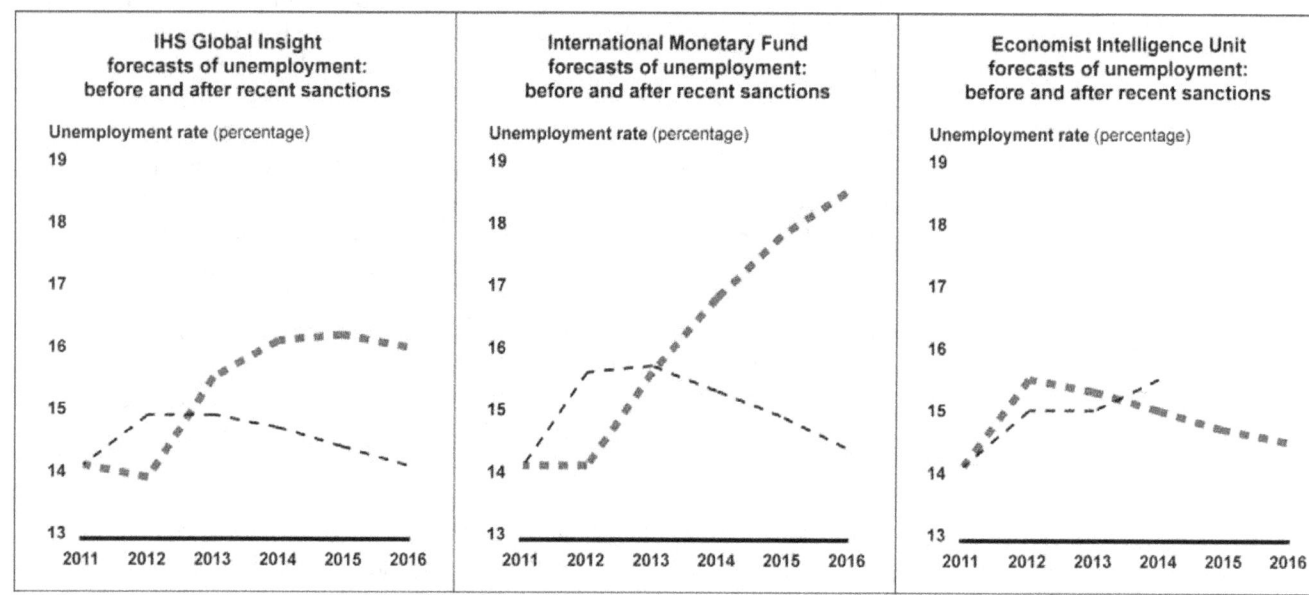

Source: GAO analysis of data from IHS Global Insight, the International Monetary Fund's World Economic Outlook, and the Economist Intelligence Unit.

Before the enactment of the recent U.S. and international sanctions, the three forecasters projected from 2012 through 2016, the unemployment rate would average between 14.6 and 15.2 percent. After the enactment of recent U.S. and international sanctions from 2010 through 2012, the forecasters predicted a higher average unemployment rate for 2012 through 2016, ranging from an average of 15.0 to 16.6 percent. All three forecasters anticipated a sustained high unemployment rate of 15 percent or higher. For example, the IMF forecast predicts an increase of unemployment to almost 19 percent in 2016.

EU and U.S. Exports of Humanitarian Goods to Iran Increased During 2012

Our analysis indicates that EU and U.S. exports of humanitarian goods to Iran increased by about 35 percent in the first 10 months of 2012, from $1.671 billion in the first 10 months of 2011 to $2.258 billion in the first 10 months of 2012 (see table 3). The increase is largely due to U.S. exports of wheat and EU exports of wheat and barley. Medicine and medical devices have remained relatively stable for the EU, but U.S. exports of those goods declined by approximately 11 percent in the first 10 months of 2012. However, the United States has not been a major supplier of humanitarian goods to Iran. U.S. exports of humanitarian goods to Iran are about 10 percent of the EU humanitarian exports to Iran.

Table 3: EU and U.S. Exports of Humanitarian Goods to Iran for the First 10 Months of 2011 and 2012

(In millions of dollars)

	January-October 2011			January-October 2012		
	Agricultural goods	Medicine and medical devices	Total	Agricultural goods	Medicine and medical devices	Total
EU[a] exports	417	1,107	**1,524**	924	1,143	**2,066**
U.S. exports	101	46	**147**	150	41	**192**
Total exports	**518**	**1,153**	**1,671**	**1,074**	**1,184**	**2,258**

Source: GAO analysis of U.S. and EU trade data.

[a]The EU data includes all 27 current member states. We used the Iranian Transactions Regulations as of October 2011 to define agriculture goods as including items that are intended to be consumed by and provide nutrition to humans or animals in Iran, including vitamins and minerals, bottled drinking water, and seeds that germinate into items that are intended to be consumed by, and provide nutrition, to humans or animals in Iran. These agricultural goods do not include alcoholic beverages, cigarettes, gum, or fertilizer. Medicines and medical devices consist of medical supplies, equipment, instruments, ambulances, and medicines, which include prescription and over-the-counter medicines for humans and animals. We use a U.S. Census-defined concordance between the North American Industry Classification System used by the United States and the Harmonized Commodity Description and Coding System used by the EU. For a more detailed discussion of our methodology, see appendix I.

Since the enactment of recent U.S. and international sanctions from 2010 through 2012, the annualized growth rate in EU exports of humanitarian goods to between 2010 and 2012 Iran nearly tripled to 18.5 percent from the historical average of 6.6 percent in 2004 through 2009 (see fig. 9). In addition, from 2010 through the third quarter of 2012, EU exports of medicine and medical devices grew at an annualized rate of about 11.2 percent, compared with about 0.6 percent from 2004 through 2009. Moreover, EU exports of agricultural goods grew at an annualized rate of 31 percent from 2010 through the third quarter of 2012. In addition, U.S. humanitarian exports to Iran increased at an annualized rate of about 10 percent since 2010 (see fig. 10). EU and U.S. agricultural exports increased in the second half of 2008, owing to increased wheat exports that assisted Iran in coping with a drought that had affected its agricultural sector.

Figure 9: EU Exports of Humanitarian Goods to Iran, First Quarter 2004 through Third Quarter 2012

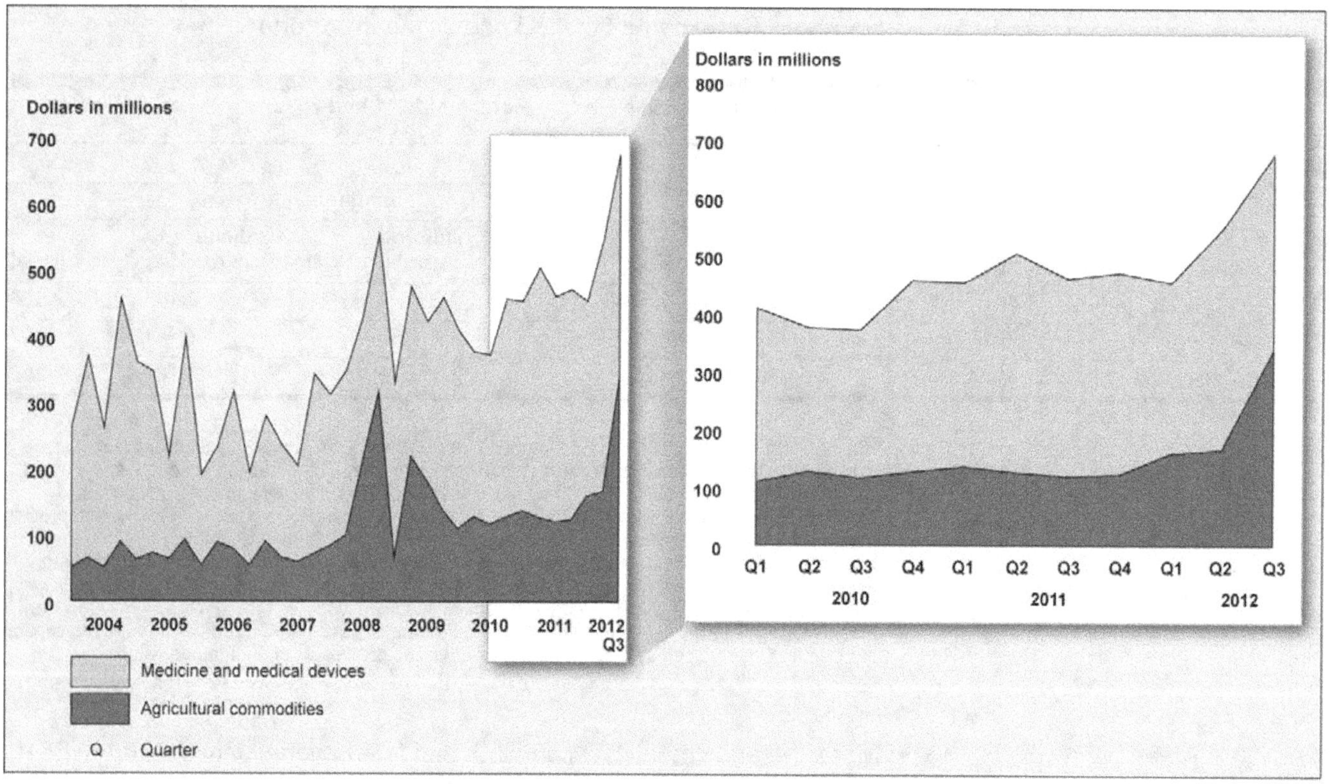

Source: GAO analysis of EU trade data

Note: The EU data includes all 27 current member states. We used the Iranian Transactions Regulations as of October 2011 to define agricultural goods and medicines and medical devices. We used a U.S. Census-defined concordance between the North American Industry Classification System used by the United States and the Harmonized Commodity Description and Coding System used by the EU. For a more detailed discussion of our methodology, see appendix I.

Figure 10: U.S. Exports of Humanitarian Goods to Iran, First Quarter 2004 through Third Quarter 2012

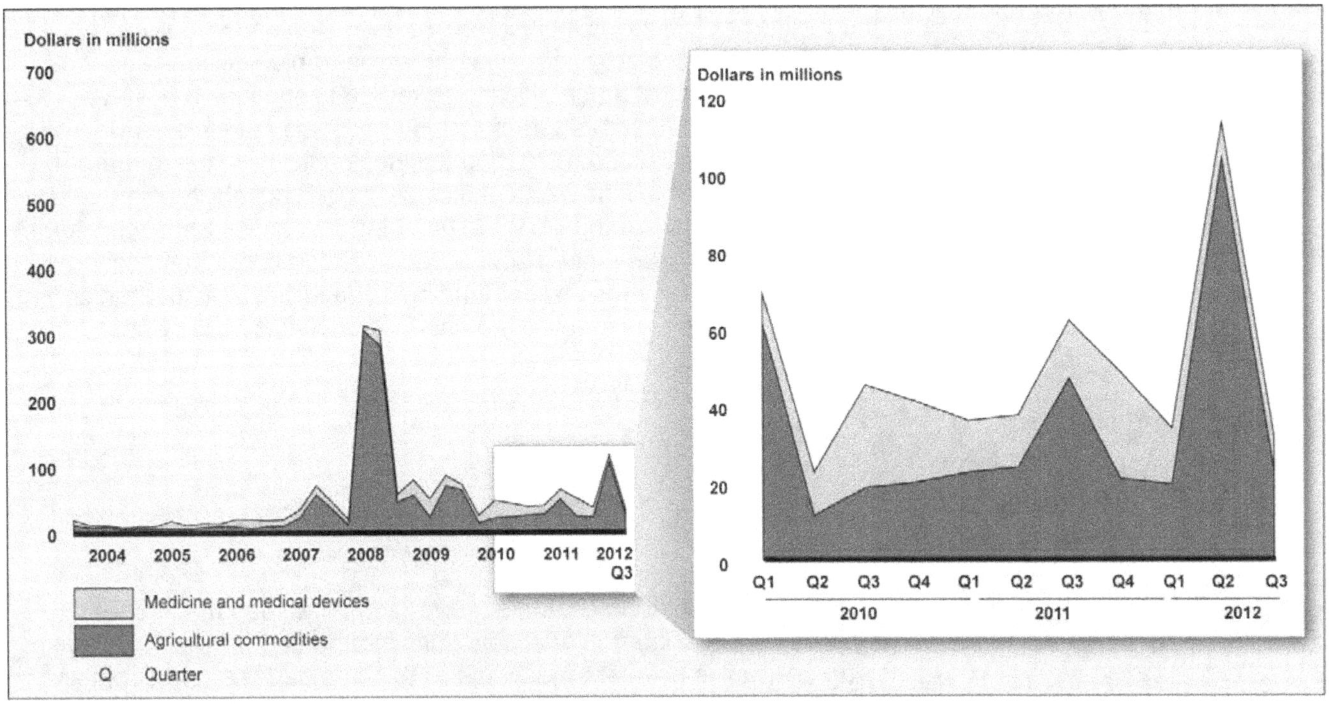

Source: GAO analysis of U.S. trade data

Note: We used the Iranian Transactions Regulations as of October 2011 to define agricultural commodities and medicines and medical devices. We used a U.S. Census-defined concordance between the North American Industry Classification System used by the United States and the Harmonized Commodity Description and Coding System used by the EU. For a more detailed discussion of our methodology, see appendix I.

Official UN and open source reports have raised concerns regarding the availability of humanitarian goods in Iran as a result of the U.S. and international sanctions. According to a 2012 UN report, the sanctions targeting Iran have had significant impacts on the general population, including causing a shortage of necessary items, such as medicines.[82] The UN also reported that some nongovernmental organizations operating in Iran have reported that people do not have access to life-saving medicines. In addition, a report published by the Wilson Center in

---

[82]UN General Assembly, "Situation of human rights in the Islamic Republic of Iran: Report to the Secretary-General," A/67/327 (Aug. 22, 2012), accessed February 15, 2013, http://www.unhcr.org/refworld/docid/50a107f02.html.

February 2013 stated that sanctions are "causing disruptions in the supply of medicine and medical equipment in Iran."[83] Foreign financial and business officials in Dubai informed us in September 2012 that sanctions may have adversely affected some Iranian citizens and businesses. Some of these officials stated that sanctions may have limited the export of some humanitarian goods, such as food and medicine, to Iran. For example, one business official indicated that the recent financial sanctions had significantly limited his ability to export food to Iran because foreign banks were unwilling to process transactions for Iranian business. Some open source reports have noted that economic mismanagement and insufficient funding for medicines by the Iranian government have exacerbated the shortage of medicines in Iran.

Iran Is Trying to Adapt to Sanctions by Seeking New Payment Mechanisms and Changing Trading Partners

Iran Is Reportedly Using Barter Agreements for Some Oil Exports

According to open sources, the government of Iran has made efforts to adapt to U.S. and international sanctions in a number of ways, including using alternative payment mechanisms such as barter agreements and changing its trading partners. Open sources report that Iran is selling oil at a discount to a number of customers, and is accepting other countries' currencies as payment, which may limit its ability to use the revenue for anything other than purchasing products in those countries. For example, open sources reported Iran has entered into barter agreements with countries including India, exchanging oil for food, medicine, and commercial products in lieu of using traditional payment methods. According to an international energy market expert, while the barter arrangements allow Iran to continue selling oil to other countries without accessing the international financial institutions, such arrangements may also limit Iran's ability to receive the full market value of its oil.[84]

[83]Siamak Namazi, "Sanctions and Medical Supply Shortages in Iran," Viewpoints 20 (Washington, D.C.: Wilson Center, 2013).

[84]According to Treasury, entities that engage in barter arrangements may be subject to U.S. sanctions to the extent that those arrangements involve entities such as a financial institution or the National Iranian Oil Company.

Furthermore, as the EU and some countries, such as South Korea and Japan, have significantly reduced the purchase of Iranian oil in response to EU and U.S. sanctions, open source reports indicate that Iran has attempted to reach agreements with India, Pakistan, and other countries to purchase Iranian oil. However, these recent agreements have thus far not fully offset the reduced exports to the EU and others. According to open source reports, the International Energy Agency stated that Iranian oil exports declined from about 2.5 million barrels per day in 2011 to about 1.3 million barrels per day in October 2012.

Iran Trading Partners Have Changed as Overall Trade Has Increased since 2010

Although Iranian exports of oil have declined, trade data from certain countries show that their exports to Iran have increased since before 2010. In 2008 and 2009, before the enactment of recent U.S. sanctions and international sanctions in 2010 through 2012, the average aggregate quarterly exports to Iran were about $15.5 billion. During the first half of 2012, quarterly exports to Iran from the same countries were $20.4 billion despite the recent U.S. and international financial sanctions targeting Iran. Table 4 shows that the share of EU exports to Iran has decreased while the shares of Turkish and United Arab Emirati exports have markedly increased. The U.S. share of Iran's imports has remained at 1 percent or less.

Table 4: Aggregate Average Quarterly Exports to Iran by Country, January 2008 to June 2012

	2008-2009		2010-2011		2012[a]	
	Dollar amount (millions)	Share (percent)	Dollar amount (millions)	Share (percent)	Dollar amount (millions)	Share (percent)
European Union	3,900.6	25	3,486.0	17	$2,200.0	11
United Arab Emirates	3,112.6	20	5,841.1	29	6,778.3	33
China	1,996.3	13	3,236.8	16	2,571.7	13
South Korea	1,041.8	7	1,334.4	7	1,708.5	8
Russian Federation	762.6	5	828.9	4	444.7	2
India	532.5	3	635.5	3	600.3	3
Turkey	506.8	3	829.2	4	2,943.8	14
Japan	444.6	3	472.6	2	167.6	1
United States	120.6	1	54.7	0	79.7	0
All Others	3,105.7	20	3,349.2	17	2,915.0	14
Total	**15,524.1**	**100**	**20,068.3**	**100**	**20,409.5**	**100**

Source: GAO analysis of MF's Direction of Trade data.

Note: Numbers may not sum to total and percentages may not sum to 100 percent because of rounding

[a]Data for 2012 cover the first two quarters of the year.

Agency Comments

We provided a draft of our report to Treasury, State, Justice, the Board of Governors of the Federal Reserve, the Office of the Comptroller of the Currency, and the International Monetary Fund for their review and comment. The agencies and organizations did not provide official comments on the report. The Departments of Treasury, the Board of Governors of the Federal Reserve, the Office of the Comptroller of the Currency, and the International Monetary Fund provided technical comments on the draft, which we incorporated in the report, as appropriate.

We are sending copies of this report to interested congressional committees, the secretaries and agency heads of the departments addressed in this report, and other interested parties. In addition, the report is available at no charge on the GAO website at http://www.gao.gov.

If you or your staff have any questions about this report, please contact me at (202) 512-9601 or melitot@gao.gov. Contact points for our Offices of Congressional Relations and Public Affairs may be found on the last page of this report. GAO staff who made key contributions to this report are listed in appendix V.

Sincerely yours,

Thomas Melito
Director
International Affairs and Trade

Appendix I: Scope and Methodology

To describe recent laws and executive orders that have added to the Department of Treasury's (Treasury) authority to implement financial sanctions targeting Iran, we reviewed the public laws and executive orders that define these sanctions, as well as the regulations developed to administer them. We spoke with Treasury officials to identify laws enacted and executive orders issued from 2010 through 2012 that added to Treasury's authority to administer and enforce financial sanctions targeting Iran. Treasury officials identified four primary laws and four executive orders that authorized the financial sanctions targeting Iran. We focused primarily on those financial sanctions targeting Iran that are defined in laws, regulations, or executive orders and that either (1) block the property of designated entities or (2) target a financial transaction as an action that can result in the prohibition of the opening or the prohibition or imposition of strict conditions on the maintenance of a correspondent or payable-through account in the United States by a foreign financial institution. We discussed the sanctions with officials from Treasury and the Department of State (State), and we reviewed official statements and press releases on the content and purpose of the sanctions. We also reviewed selected financial sanctions targeting Iran enacted by the United Nations (UN) and European Union (EU).

To describe U.S. efforts to administer U.S. financial sanctions targeting Iran, we reviewed Treasury regulations and guidance establishing the process for administering the sanctions. We reviewed the Iranian Financial Sanctions Regulations,[1] Iranian Transactions and Sanctions Regulations,[2] and additional sanctions guidance and documents developed and published by Treasury. We spoke with Treasury officials to discuss the agency's administration of financial sanctions through various activities, including its development of regulations, outreach to banks and financial institutions, review of financial transactions, identification of potential violations, and assessment of the impact of financial sanctions. We also interviewed State officials regarding the department's process for granting exceptions under section 1245 of the National Defense Authorization Act of 2012.[3] To describe the efforts of the U.S. government and banks to ensure compliance with the financial sanctions targeting

---

[1] 31 C.F.R. pt. 561.

[2] 31 C.F.R. pt. 560.

[3] Pub. L. No. 112-81, § 1245(d).

Iran, we reviewed the Bank Secrecy Act, as amended,[4] and the examination procedures used by the regulators to assess banks' compliance with Bank Secrecy Act and Office of Foreign Assets Control-related requirements, which includes guidance on the establishment and maintenance of an effective Office of Foreign Assets Control (OFAC) compliance program.[5] We also reviewed available data from the regulators on the numbers of Bank Secrecy Act examinations conducted during fiscal years 2010–2012, which generally included reviews of banks' OFAC compliance programs. We interviewed officials from the Board of Governors for the Federal Reserve System and the Office of the Comptroller of the Currency to discuss the bank examination process regarding OFAC compliance programs. We also spoke with representatives from the American Bankers Association and the Institute of International Bankers to discuss the role that banks play in the administration of financial sanctions and the programs that banks establish to comply with OFAC reporting guidelines.

To describe U.S. efforts to enforce financial sanctions targeting Iran, we interviewed officials from Treasury, State, the Department of Justice (Justice), and federal banking regulatory agencies to identify the methods and activities that the agencies used for enforcement. We reviewed the Specially Designated Nationals list, which Treasury publishes, to determine the number of entities that Treasury designated for violations of U.S. financial sanctions targeting Iran. We reviewed OFAC guidance on the enforcement of financial sanctions. We also reviewed documents on the federal banking regulators' enforcement actions against banks involving OFAC compliance issues. We additionally reviewed court documents and press releases regarding enforcement actions taken by Justice in response to banks' criminal violations of financial sanctions.

To assess Iranian economic performance, we identified a group of peer economies, which helped us to isolate economic changes that are unique to Iran but not necessarily to identify the impact of sanctions. The peer group we identified includes the International Monetary Fund's (IMF) Middle East and North Africa region, neighboring countries not included in

---

[4]12 U.S.C. §§ 1829b, 1951-1959; 31 U.S.C. §§ 5311 et seq.

[5]Federal and state banking regulatory agencies issued a Bank Secrecy Act/Anti-Money Laundering Manual that includes the regulators' expectations regarding banks' OFAC compliance programs. (www.ffiec.gov.bsa/bsa_aml_infbase/default.htm. pp.147-159)

the Middle East and North Africa region, and oil export-dependent countries outside the region. The peer group is comprised of Algeria, Angola, Armenia, Azerbaijan, Bahrain, Djibouti, Egypt, Equatorial Guinea, Gabon, Jordan, Kuwait, Mauritania, Morocco, Oman, Panama, Republic of Congo, Qatar, Saudi Arabia, Tunisia, Turkey, Turkmenistan, United Arab Emirates, and Venezuela. The group excludes Afghanistan, Chad, Iraq, Lebanon, Libya, Nigeria, Pakistan, Sudan, Syria, and Yemen—countries that were rated very high on the Fund for Peace Failed States Index or very low on the Institute for Economics and Peace Global Peace Index in 2011 or 2012. We assessed the performance of the Iranian oil market (oil production and oil export revenue), gross domestic product, and consumer price inflation against the peer group's, using data from IMF databases (World Economic Outlook and International Financial Statistics), the Energy Information Administration (International Energy Statistics database), IHS Global Insight, and the Economist Intelligence Unit. We assessed the reliability of these data and found that they were sufficiently reliable for identifying peers for the Iranian economy and assessing Iran's economic performance. For example, we corroborated data from multiple sources and spoke with cognizant officials and experts to confirm the reliability of the data. Because of concerns about Iranian economic data, we relied on third party data and estimates to a large extent, and considered the published views of the IMF on Iranian inflation data, whose original source was the Central Bank of Iran. If, as some suggest, Iranian official statistics underestimate inflation, our results with respect to inflation are conservative. In addition to conducting simple peer comparisons, we conducted a more rigorous econometric analysis that controlled for historical trends in Iranian oil production as well as contemporaneous changes in peers' oil production. We interpreted the results of our analysis in light of expert views, contemporaneous events including U.S. and EU sanctions, and certain domestic policies in Iran. In most instances we did not attempt to isolate the impact of U.S. financial sanctions. The contemporaneous implementation of many sanctions, including U.S., UN, and EU financial and non-financial sanctions from 2010 through 2012, would make attributing certain outcomes to any particular sanction very difficult. For a complete description of our peer group selection and econometric analysis see Appendix III.

To assess the impact of the sanctions on the projected future performance of the Iranian economy, we reviewed the forecasts that three sources–the IMF's World Economic Outlook, IHS Global Insight, and Economist Intelligence Unit–developed to predict the performance of Iran's economy from 2012 through 2016. We reviewed the forecasts that each source developed before the enactment of the most recent U.S. and international sanctions, and we compared the results with forecasts published between September and October 2012 to identify changes in the predicted performance of the Iranian economy. To compile the original forecasts, we used IHS Global Insight data for June 2010 and the IMF World Economic Outlook estimates for April 2010, with the exception of predicted unemployment rate, which came from the September 2011 World Economic Outlook database. We also averaged two forecasts developed by the Economist Intelligence Unit, from March 2010 and October 2010, to establish a baseline forecast of the performance of Iran's economy before the enactment of the recent sanctions. For the updated forecasts, we used the November 2012 IHS Global Insight data, the October 2012 IMF World Economic Outlook database, and the November 2012 Economist Intelligence Unit forecasts.

To identify the efforts of the government of Iran to adapt to the U.S. and international sanctions, we reviewed U.S. government statements regarding the impact of sanctions on Iran in publicly available testimonies, speeches, and other remarks made by U.S. officials from State, Treasury, and the White House. We reviewed these statements regarding the U.S. government's position on the impact of sanctions on Iran, factors that might lessen their impact, the influence of international sanctions on the impact of sanctions, and for ways that Iran was adapting to the sanctions. We interviewed U.S. government officials, as well as academic and independent experts, regarding the extent to which sanctions targeting Iran have affected the Iranian economy and government and business with Iran. In addition, we reviewed open source and media reports regarding the effect of U.S. and international sanctions on Iran.

To review the impact of sanctions targeting Iran on the availability of humanitarian goods to Iran, we reviewed official UN and open source reports about the access of such goods in Iran. In addition, since the United Arab Emirates is one of Iran's largest trading partners, we met with several business officials in Dubai, United Arab Emirates, to discuss the effect that sanctions have had on business with Iran and the resulting impact on Iranian citizens and the availability of humanitarian goods. To analyze the export of humanitarian goods to Iran, we analyzed U.S. and EU trade data between January 2004 and October 2012. For the purposes of this report, we defined "humanitarian goods" as those goods authorized for exports by the Iranian Transactions Regulations as of October 2011. The regulations defined agriculture goods to include items that are intended to be consumed by and provide nutrition to humans or animals in Iran, including vitamins and minerals, bottled drinking water, and seeds that germinate into items that are intended to be consumed by and provide nutrition to humans or animals in Iran. Agricultural goods did not include alcoholic beverages, cigarettes, gum, or fertilizer. Medicine and medical devices consisted of medical supplies, equipment, instruments, and ambulances, and medicines which include prescription and over-the-counter medicines for humans and animals. We used a U.S. Census-defined concordance between the North American Industry Classification System used by the United States and the Harmonized Commodity Description and Coding System used by the European Union. We performed our selection of humanitarian goods at the two-, four- and five-digit levels of the harmonized system codes, as appropriate. For the trend analysis since January 2004, we also performed a sensitivity check by using the definition of authorized agricultural exports to Iran stated in the Export Administration Regulations as of July 2001. These regulations included tobacco and tobacco products, beer, wine and spirits, livestock, fertilizer and reproductive materials in the list of authorized agricultural exports. We found that those categories of products did not have a significant impact on our analysis, and we decided to use a consistent definition for our short-term 10-month comparison between 2011 and 2012 exports, as well as our longer-term trend analysis. In addition, the narrower scope of the authorized agricultural exports as stated in the updated regulations provided a more precise definition of humanitarian goods. To ensure that we did not overlook any authorized agricultural commodities and medicine and medical devices exported by the U.S. to Iran, we also reviewed OFAC data of export licenses issued to U.S. businesses that allowed the export of these goods to Iran between 2009 and 2012.

We conducted this performance audit from February 2012 to February 2013 in accordance with generally accepted government auditing standards. Those standards require that we plan and perform the audit to obtain sufficient, appropriate evidence to provide a reasonable basis for our findings and conclusions based on our audit objectives. We believe that the evidence obtained provides a reasonable basis for our findings and conclusions based on our audit objectives.

Appendix II: Selected U.S. and International Sanctions Targeting Iran

Figure 11: Selected U.S. and International Sanctions Targeting Iran 1984 through 2007

Selected U.S. government sanctions	2007 to 1984	Selected international actions
	2007	• **Mar:** UNSC resolution 1747 required Iran to suspend enrichment. This resolution widened the scope of UNSC resolution 1737 by banning Iran's arms exports and by freezing the assets of, and restricting travel by, designated individuals engaged in the country's proliferation-sensitive nuclear activities. • **May:** IAEA reports that Iran had not suspended its uranium enrichment activities and had continued operation of its pilot fuel enrichment plant.
• **Sept:** The Iran Freedom Support Act amended the Iran and Libya Sanctions Act to (1) add support of Iran's ability to acquire nuclear, chemical, biological, advanced conventional weapons as sanctionable and (2) remove Libya from the Iran and Libya Sanctions Act (renamed Iran Sanctions Act). • **Oct:** The North Korea Nonproliferation Act of 2006 amended the Iran and Syria Nonproliferation Act to include North Korea (renaming it the Iran, North Korea, Syria Nonproliferation Act).	2006	• **Jan:** Iran resumed enrichment activities. • **Feb:** IAEA voted for a resolution to report Iran to UNSC. • **July:** UNSC resolution 1696 called for Iran to suspend all uranium enrichment–related activities and uranium-reprocessing activities. • **Dec:** UNSC resolution 1737 required Iran to suspend its uranium enrichment and reprocessing activities as requested under resolution 1696 and required that all states take measures to prevent the supply, sales or transfer of all items, goods and technology that could contribute to Iran's enrichment-related activities or development of nuclear weapon delivery systems.
• **Nov:** The Iran Nonproliferation Amendments Act of 2005 amended the Iran Nonproliferation Act of 2000 to include Syria (renaming it the Iran and Syria Nonproliferation Act).	2005	• **Aug:** Iran broke the seals on its uranium conversion facility in its Isfahan plant; IAEA called on Iran to suspend enrichment-related activities.
	2004	• **Nov:** Under the Paris Agreement with the EU 3 (Britain, France, and Germany), Iran agreed to suspend enrichment in exchange for renewed trade talks.
	2003	• **June:** IAEA stated that Iran had failed to report certain nuclear materials and activities and requested cooperation from Iran.
	2002	
	2001	
• **Mar:** The Iran Nonproliferation Act of 2000 imposed sanctions against foreign persons transferring controlled goods to Iran or engaging in proliferation activities (nuclear, biological, or chemical weapons or ballistic or cruise missile systems) with Iran. • **Apr:** Restrictions were lifted on certain (1) U.S. imports of Iranian goods such as carpets, dried fruits, and nuts and (2) U.S. exports to Iran such as food, agricultural commodities, medicine, or medical equipment.	2000	
	1999	
	1998	
• **Aug:** EO 13059 prohibited certain transactions with respect to Iran and confirmed the trade and investment activities ban against Iran.	1997	
• **Aug:** The Iran and Libya Sanctions Act of 1996 imposed sanctions against parties that invest $40 million or more in the development of Iran's petroleum resources. After the first year, sanctions shall be applied to nationals of nonwaiver countries that invest $20 million or more.	1996	
• **Mar:** EO 12957 restricted U.S. involvement with the development of Iran's petroleum resources. • **May:** EO 12959 banned U.S. imports of Iranian goods, U.S. exports to Iran, and U.S. investment in Iran.	1995	
	1994	
	1993	
• **Oct:** The Iran-Iraq Arms Nonproliferation Act of 1992 imposed sanctions against foreign parties that contribute to Iran's efforts to acquire destabilizing numbers and types of conventional weapons.	1992	
	1991	
	1990	
	1989	
	1988	
• **Oct:** EO 12613 banned U.S. imports of Iranian goods.	1987	
	1986	
	1985	
• **Jan:** Iran was designated a "state sponsor of terrorism."	1984	

Source: GAO analysis of U.S. laws and executive orders, as well as UN documents, including UN Security Council resolutions.

Appendix III: Econometric Analysis of Iran Economic Indicators

In this appendix we describe the process we used to identify peers for the Iranian economy, the econometric approach we used to determine the magnitude and statistical significance of recent changes in several economic indicators for Iran, and the results of this analysis.

Peer Identification

To help understand economic changes occurring uniquely in Iran we identified a set of peer countries to approximate a control group. We identified (1) regional peers, and (2) oil exporting peers, and then we pooled the two groups to form a single peer group. To identify regional peers, we chose countries in the International Monetary Fund's (IMF) Middle East and North Africa peer group and other countries that bordered Iran but were not in the group. To identify countries whose dependence on oil exports is similar to Iran's, we calculated Iran's oil exports as a percentage of goods exports (roughly 86 percent), and then considered any country to be an oil exporting peer if its oil exports were more than 75 percent of goods exports.

To remove certain countries that experienced significant instability associated with civil conflict or political violence (e.g., certain countries associated with the "Arab Spring"), we excluded countries from the peer group if they exceeded certain thresholds on the Fund for Peace Failed States Index or the Institute for Economics and Peace Global Peace Index in 2011 or 2012.[1] We then combined into a single peer group the countries that we had identified with both methodologies (see table 5).

[1]For the Failed States index, we excluded potential peers whose score exceeded 100 (out of 120). For the Global Peace Index, we excluded potential peers whose score exceeded 2.5 (out of 5). Based on these criteria we excluded Afghanistan, Chad, Iraq, Lebanon, Libya, Nigeria, Pakistan, Sudan, Syria, and Yemen.

Table 5: Peers for the Iranian Economy

Peer country	Type
Algeria	Regional and oil exporting peer
Angola	Oil exporting peer
Armenia	Regional peer
Azerbaijan	Regional and oil exporting peer
Bahrain	Regional peer
Djibouti	Regional peer
Egypt	Regional peer
Equatorial Guinea	Oil exporting peer
Gabon	Oil exporting peer
Jordan	Regional peer
Kuwait	Regional and oil exporting peer
Mauritania	Regional peer
Morocco	Regional peer
Oman	Regional peer
Panama	Oil exporting peer
Qatar	Regional and oil exporting peer
Republic of Congo	Oil exporting peer
Saudi Arabia	Regional and oil exporting peer
Tunisia	Regional peer
Turkey	Regional peer
Turkmenistan	Regional peer
United Arab Emirates	Regional peer
Venezuela	Oil exporting peer

Source: GAO analysis of International Monetary Fund data.

Econometric Approach

We estimated several panel data difference-in-difference models on the growth rates of two macroeconomic indicators: oil production and consumer prices. While the dependent variable varies, the independent variables are the same across models—an intercept and month and country fixed effects. We assume a robust covariance structure which allows for heteroskedasticity–volatility could vary over time or across countries–and serial correlation of the errors within a country. In addition, we estimate two variations based on different "sanctions dummies" for Iran that correspond to two key financial sanctions laws—Comprehensive Iran Sanctions, Accountability, and Divestment Act of 2010 (CISADA), passed in July 2010, and the National Defense Authorization Act for

Fiscal Year 2012 (NDAA), passed in December 2011 (As a result, the post-sanction dummies are equal to 1 for observations on Iran from August 2010 to the present in the case of CISADA and from January 2012 to the present in the case of NDAA). For the NDAA dummy in particular, we recognize that European Union (EU) sanctions related to insurance and an EU oil embargo are contemporaneous with NDAA financial sanctions. Furthermore, we recognize that we are not identifying the impact of sanctions based on this approach. We do not control for other macroeconomic or idiosyncratic (time-country specific) factors. We also recognize that we lack detailed institutional knowledge of idiosyncratic factors across all of the countries in our sample. However, we argue that other factors we might attempt to control for are likely to be endogenous to the sanctions. For example, one would typically include the growth of the money supply and the output gap in a regression designed to explain inflation. However, both of these factors could be influenced by the sanctions or by policy responses to the sanctions; therefore, by including them we could underestimate the role of sanctions.

We estimated all models with data from February 2000 to the most recently available month at the time of the analysis (June 2012 or July 2012).

Results

Changes in the Iranian economic indicators we analyzed were consistently statistically significant during the time period associated with recent U.S. financial sanctions, and the measured effects (coefficients) were of magnitudes that were economically meaningful. The size of the effect is larger in the post-NDAA time period (which also includes EU sanctions related to oil and insurance) than in the post-CISADA period. Although this is not necessarily a measure of the impact of U.S. and international sanctions, it does indicate that the recent deterioration in the Iranian economy is larger than what one would expect relative to the historical trends and volatility of Iran and its peers.[2]

---

[2]For our econometric analysis as well as graphical comparisons of Iran with peers, we included only countries for which data for the full time period were available at the time of our analysis. This resulted in the exclusion of some peers in each analysis or comparison.

The increase in the inflation rate is statistically significant and large, indicating that inflation is significantly larger than one would expect during the post-CISADA and post-NDAA time periods (see table 6). The effect in 2012 (the post-NDAA period) is slightly larger: 12.6 percentage points versus 10.2 percentage points in the post-CISADA period. An energy subsidy program initiated in December 2010 is likely to have contributed to higher inflation during this time period. U.S. and international sanctions may have contributed to higher transaction costs, higher import prices, and a lower exchange rate, all of which could increase inflation.

Table 6: Inflation Difference-in-Difference Model

Sanctions period	Coefficient (p-value)	Annualized effect
Post-CISADA change	0.0082 (0.0001)	10.24%
Post-NDAA change	0.0099 (<0.0001)	12.57%

Source: GAO analysis of International Monetary Fund data.

Note: In addition to indicators for Iran in the post-CISADA or post-NDAA time periods, models are estimated with an intercept, month and country fixed effects. CISADA and NDAA models estimated independently.

The decline in oil production is also statistically significant and large, indicating that oil production fell significantly more than one would expect during the post-CISADA and post-NDAA time periods (see table 7). The effect in 2012 (the post-NDAA period) is much larger: 26 percentage points versus 9 percentage points in the post-CISADA period. U.S. and international sanctions, such as a European Union embargo on oil from Iran, may have made it more difficult to attract investment in Iran's oil sector, more difficult to sell oil on international markets, and more difficult to receive payment for oil Iran was able to sell, all of which could decrease oil production.

Table 7: Oil Production Difference-in-Difference Model

Sanctions period	Coefficient (p-value)	Annualized effect
Post-CISADA change	-0.0078 (<0.0001)	-8.98%
Post-NDAA change	-0.0244 (<0.0001)	-25.64%

Source: GAO analysis of Energy Information Administration data.

Note: In addition to indicators for Iran in the post-CISADA or post-NDAA time periods, models are estimated with an intercept, month and country fixed effects. CISADA and NDAA models estimated independently.

We estimated several additional models to assess the robustness of our results. In one instance, we allowed the Iran dummy variables representing the post-CISADA and post-NDAA time periods to vary over time, beginning in January 2010. The coefficients on the dummy variables were larger and more likely to be statistically significant during the post-CISADA and, especially, post-NDAA time periods. We also estimated models with alternative error structures that allow for more general heteroskedasticity or for contemporaneous correlation across countries, respectively, and our results were substantively unchanged.

Appendix IV: IAEA Reports on the Development of the Iranian Nuclear Program

Iran's initial efforts to develop nuclear energy technology began in the 1950s with assistance from the United States through President Eisenhower's Atoms for Peace program. Iran's nuclear energy program accelerated during the mid-1970s through the efforts of Shah Mohammad Pahlavi.[1] However, not much was publicly known of the extent of Iran's nuclear capability until 2002, when the International Atomic Energy Agency (IAEA) was informed of a previously undeclared nuclear enrichment plant in Natanz and a heavy water plant in Arak.[2] Subsequent IAEA inspections revealed that Iran had already made significant progress toward mastering the technology needed to make enriched uranium, a material that can be used to fuel nuclear weapons. IAEA inspectors reported that they were unable to conclude that Iran's program was exclusively peaceful. Under the terms of the Paris Agreement, negotiated in 2004, Iran voluntarily suspended its uranium enrichment program. In August 2005, coinciding with President Ahmadinejad's assumption of power, Iran resumed its enrichment program. In response, IAEA reported these actions to the UN Security Council (UNSC). This resulted in UNSC Resolution 1696, which demanded that Iran suspend its uranium enrichment and reprocessing activities, acting under Article 40 of the UN Charter.[3] The resolution requested that the IAEA complete a report by August 31, 2006, on whether Iran had suspended its enrichment activities. The August IAEA report concluded that Iran had not suspended its enrichment activities and had not addressed the outstanding verification issues—a conclusion that IAEA reasserted in May 2007.

In its follow-up inspection, IAEA reported that Iran had neither suspended its enrichment activities nor provided the necessary transparency to remove uncertainties associated with some of its activities. Iran continued to defy the UNSC resolutions and was sanctioned by a series of additional UNSC resolutions between 2006 and 2010 that, among other things, prohibited the sale of technology that could contribute to Iran's

---

[1]In 1968, Iran signed the Nuclear Nonproliferation Treaty, which made the peaceful application of nuclear technology available to Iran, and Iran agreed to the specific safeguards and inspection treaty in 1974.

[2]In the Arak heavy water plant, heavy water is produced by extracting heavy water from regular water. Heavy water is water in which the hydrogen atom is replaced by the deuterium isotope and it is used in certain types of nuclear reactors where plutonium is bred from natural uranium. Plutonium is used in nuclear weapons and for nuclear power production.

[3]S.C. Res. 1696, U.N. Doc. S/RES/1696 (2006).

enrichment activities and freeze financial assets of entities involved in the Iranian nuclear industry.

Beginning in 2006, six countries formed a group, the "Permanent Five Plus 1," to negotiate with Iran through a series of discussions.[4] The group has negotiated with Iran on several occasions, but, to date, has not achieved any breakthroughs or reached agreement with Iran.

A November 2011 IAEA report cited credible information that led to serious concerns indicating that Iran carried out activities relevant to the development of a nuclear explosive device and was continuing to expand its inventory of enriched uranium. Most recently, the November 2012 IAEA report stated that Iran had installed additional centrifuges and had continued to enrich uranium. In addition, the report reiterated IAEA's inability to reach agreement with Iran on a "structured approach" to resolving outstanding questions regarding the potential military dimensions to Iran's program that were cited in the November 2011 report.

---

[4]The "Permanent 5 Plus 1" group includes the five permanent members of the UN Security Council (China, France, Russia, the United Kingdom, and the United States) and Germany.

Appendix V: GAO Contact and Staff Acknowledgments

GAO Contact	Thomas Melito, (202) 512-9601 or melitot@gao.gov
Staff Acknowledgments	In addition to the contact named above, Pierre Toureille (Assistant Director), Tetsuo Miyabara (Assistant Director), John F. Miller, Eddie Uyekawa, Emily Biskup, Grace P. Lui, Michael Hoffman, Tonita Gillich, Gergana Danailova-Trainor, Jennifer Young, Debbie Chung, and Bruce Kutnick made key contributions to this report. Additional technical assistance was provided by Joanna Berry, Gezahegne Bekele, Etana Finkler, Martin De Alteriis, Fang He, Reid Lowe, Elisabeth Helmer, Emily Gupta, Roberto Pinero, Courtney LaFountain, and Heather Latta.

GAO's Mission	The Government Accountability Office, the audit, evaluation, and investigative arm of Congress, exists to support Congress in meeting its constitutional responsibilities and to help improve the performance and accountability of the federal government for the American people. GAO examines the use of public funds; evaluates federal programs and policies; and provides analyses, recommendations, and other assistance to help Congress make informed oversight, policy, and funding decisions. GAO's commitment to good government is reflected in its core values of accountability, integrity, and reliability.
Obtaining Copies of GAO Reports and Testimony	The fastest and easiest way to obtain copies of GAO documents at no cost is through GAO's website (http://www.gao.gov). Each weekday afternoon, GAO posts on its website newly released reports, testimony, and correspondence. To have GAO e-mail you a list of newly posted products, go to http://www.gao.gov and select "E-mail Updates."
Order by Phone	The price of each GAO publication reflects GAO's actual cost of production and distribution and depends on the number of pages in the publication and whether the publication is printed in color or black and white. Pricing and ordering information is posted on GAO's website, http://www.gao.gov/ordering.htm. Place orders by calling (202) 512-6000, toll free (866) 801-7077, or TDD (202) 512-2537. Orders may be paid for using American Express, Discover Card, MasterCard, Visa, check, or money order. Call for additional information.
Connect with GAO	Connect with GAO on Facebook, Flickr, Twitter, and YouTube. Subscribe to our RSS Feeds or E-mail Updates. Listen to our Podcasts. Visit GAO on the web at www.gao.gov.
To Report Fraud, Waste, and Abuse in Federal Programs	Contact: Website: http://www.gao.gov/fraudnet/fraudnet.htm E-mail: fraudnet@gao.gov Automated answering system: (800) 424-5454 or (202) 512-7470
Congressional Relations	Katherine Siggerud, Managing Director, siggerudk@gao.gov, (202) 512-4400, U.S. Government Accountability Office, 441 G Street NW, Room 7125, Washington, DC 20548
Public Affairs	Chuck Young, Managing Director, youngc1@gao.gov, (202) 512-4800 U.S. Government Accountability Office, 441 G Street NW, Room 7149 Washington, DC 20548

Please Print on Recycled Paper.